A NOTRE DAME MAN

The Life, Lore and Runs of Erick Penick

Eric Penick
Stephen Alexander
Foreword by Dave Casper

ISBN: 9798853135345
Imprint: Independently published

Library of Congress Control Number: 2018675309
Printed in the United States of America

Dedications

Eric Penick
I want to dedicate this book to all of my grandchildren. "A Notre Dame Man: The Life, Lore and Runs of Eric Penick" captures the legacy of who I am as a man, and how I became that man. I hope that my story teaches and inspires each of you.

Stephen Alexander
This book is dedicated to my daughter, Morgan Jane Mahalic. Her life began on November 18, 2022 when she came into the world six weeks early. She was my constant companion as Eric and I wrote this book. Morgan's lore is only beginning.

"Let the redeemed of the Lord tell their story."

--PSALM 107:2

FOREWORD

By
Dave Casper

In my role as captain of the 1973 Notre Dame National Championship football team, I did not tell my teammates what to do too often. I felt like I needed to watch over certain guys on the team, though. Eric Penick was one of those guys.

When I knew him at Notre Dame, Eric was either very happy or very unhappy.

If things were going well, and he was not getting yelled at by the coaches, Eric was happy. When he was getting yelled at by the coaches, Eric was a very unhappy guy.

In the 1970s, football coaches yelled. A lot. Our Notre Dame coaches, among the best of all-time, were no different. They were not just yelling at Eric, of course. I tell stories about how much our coaches yelled at me. They were indiscriminate yellers.

I could tell the yelling bothered Eric. And I could tell that he needed a little bit of a friend.

One day in practice, after the coaches hollered at Eric for a mistake, I told him, "It's just water off a duck's back, Eric."

Just a few minutes later, Eric was getting yelled at by the coaches again for something. When Eric got back to the offensive huddle, he looked at me, smiled and said, "Quack, quack, quack!"

It became a thing between us. I would quack at him if he was having a bad day. I told him that the coaches yelling at us was not to be taken personally. "Quack, quack, quack."

Eric got to the point where he could usually just laugh it off and quack back at me. "Quack, quack, quack."

That was Eric. He was a charismatic guy.

In 1973, the Irish had changed their offense from a Power-I scheme to a Wing-T system. It was a much more wide-open offense. It fit Eric's skillset well. He could make the big plays.

Eric's big plays included his historic 85-yard touchdown run against USC, and his 12-yard touchdown run against Alabama in the Sugar Bowl which effectively clinched our National Championship.

There is no doubt that the reason the coaches yelled at Eric was because they saw his enormous talent and unlimited potential.

Coach Ara Parseghian's renowned Notre Dame football program was based on precise structure and the highest values.

In my case, and I think in Eric's case, the infusion of that structure and those values were like a vaccine. Sometimes it may take a while to need the impact of the vaccine. But the structure and values were there as an inoculation to help all of us fight off bad things. Our time at Notre Dame, and the friendships we developed among our teammates, gave us a moral compass to know when we were doing the right things and when we were doing the wrong things.

Eric had some huge runs for Notre Dame. He was an unmistakably gifted athlete. Eric was also a naturally good guy. Eric's teammates all saw his value as a person. If I had not liked Eric, I probably would not have talked to him much.

Eric, though, was somebody worth talking to. His life story is one worth reading.

--Dave Casper

PROLOGUE

It was the pivotal moment of the most captivating college football game ever played. And I was going to get the ball.

Alabama led Notre Dame 17-14 with just over two and a half minutes remaining in the third quarter of the 1973 Sugar Bowl.

Seconds before, the Fighting Irish defense had stunned the Crimson Tide by forcing a turnover and returning the ball back to the Alabama 12-yard-line.

In a game filled with momentum swings and haymaker punches, the turnover had staggered the Tide and put them back on their heels. Notre Dame now needed to deliver a knockout blow to break Alabama's jaw.

As the Notre Dame offense ran onto the field, the call came in from legendary Irish coach Ara Parseghian: A high-low sweep with Eric Penick taking the handoff.

It was the same play Notre Dame had run two months earlier against USC. On that October day in South Bend, I had taken the handoff and gone 85-yards for a touchdown. The run broke the game open against the Trojans, propelling the Irish to an undefeated season and a Sugar Bowl berth against Alabama.

No one knew that I had fractured my left ankle earlier in the third quarter of the Sugar Bowl. As I lined up in my three-point stance on the right side of the field, knowing that the ball was going to me, adrenaline was coursing through my veins, and I could not even feel the injury.

The ball was snapped.

I sprinted toward the left side of the field. We faked a fullback dive, then I had the ball in my hands. When I reached the line of scrimmage, there was no one there. The offensive linemen had opened up a massive hole. I flashed through the hole and was able to stand up and accelerate right away, carrying the ball in my left arm.

I picked up not one, but *two* downfield blocks from tight end Dave Casper.

I read Casper's blocks and bounced the run to the sideline.

And then I was gone, 12-yards into the endzone, untouched.

As I crossed the goal line, I raised up my right hand in pure triumph. The extra point put Notre Dame up 21-17 with 2:30 remaining in the third quarter.

Less than an hour later, the final whistle blew. Notre Dame had defeated Alabama 24-23, winning the 1973 National Championship.

I was 20-years-old. I was a star junior running back for the Notre Dame Fighting Irish. That season, I had scored two of the most important touchdowns in the storied history of Notre Dame football. I had a dazzlingly bright future ahead of me in the NFL.

As I celebrated with my teammates that night, I could have never believed that that touchdown against Alabama would be the last time I ever crossed the goal line and stood in the end zone.

The ankle I had fractured in the Sugar Bowl never fully healed. I was too tough to tell anyone that it was still bothering me, though.

In a spring practice in 1974, just a few months after the Irish had won the National Championship, I took a handoff on another high-low-sweep. I was hit by two teammates. My ankle bent under me and I felt it snap clean through.

In 1974, the treatment for a badly broken ankle was something out of the stone age. The doctors sliced me open and filled the joint with screws to keep it together. I was never again the same running back, nor the same man.

I came back and played a little my senior year, and I had enough potential that I was a late round draft pick by the Denver Broncos. I played in the 1975 NFL preseason, but I no longer had the burst of speed I had once had, and I did not make the final roster.

That broken ankle changed my life. It changed my whole life. I was a different person after I got hurt. I went from being happy-go-lucky all the time to just being bitter and sad and mean.

The injury would eventually lead me down a path that saw me spend four and a half years in prison. Then, years later, long after I had found my redemption inside the walls of my prison cell, complications from that ankle injury, combined with diabetes, forced my doctors to amputate my left leg above my knee.

During my time at Notre Dame, I once had a candid conversation with Ara Parseghian.

"Coach," I said, "what kind of man will I be when I leave Notre Dame?"

"I don't know right now, Eric," Coach Parseghian said. "You haven't had any adversity in your life. Everything has been handed to you. Everything has been good for you. I can tell you about the guys who aren't playing and what kind of guys they are. But you, I just don't know yet."

Well, I went through adversity. I lost football. I lost my freedom. And finally, I lost my leg.

Through it all, though, I rose again and again. I walked straight through hell so that I could feel the light of heaven upon my face.

Years later, Ara and I had another conversation.

"Eric," Coach Parseghian said, "I can see it now. Before, I didn't know what kind of man you would be because you always had it made as a football player and in life. I can see the adversity you went through now, though. You learned how to persevere in good times and bad times. Now, I can tell what kind of a man you are by the obstacles you've overcome. I know what kind of man you are, Eric. You are a good man."

Hearing Coach Parseghian say those words, after everything I had been through, that made all the difference in the world to me.

In the end, I did become a good man.

I became a Notre Dame Man.

It was like another lifetime ago, but this is how I remember it all happening.

CHAPTER 1

I did not grow up rich, but I was well-rounded. My childhood was filled with education, sports, religion, and music.

I was born at Mt. Sinai Hospital in Cleveland, Ohio, on September 21, 1953. It is an auspicious birthday as years later, in the song "September," Earth Wind and Fire sang, "Do you remember, the 21st night of September?"

The 1950s were a totally different time in America. Growing up, my family and I called ourselves Negroes.

My mother, Bertha Moon, worked as a GS-11 contract expeditor for the government. She was cool, and she was very smart. Being Black, it was hard for her to be as successful as she was. But my mother, I cannot say this enough, she was dynamic. She once got promoted and was given a bonus for streamlining how contracts were signed with carbon copies, making it more efficient and saving the government a bunch of money.

My mother was working all the time. She had to work to take care of her family.

My stepfather, Thomas Moon, had a job as a machine setup operator. He was always working too. I called my stepfather "Dad," all my life. He was my father.

I did not get to know my birth-father, Mose Penick, or his side of the family, until I was in college.

My sister, Mosetta Penick, was named after our birth-father. She was six years older than me.

When my mother remarried, I got two stepbrothers. Pat Moon was much older, and I never really got to know him. Tommy Moon was still a lot older than me, but he came around. He used to mess with me all the time, sit on my head, and do all kinds of stuff. We were close. I finally had a big brother.

I was eight-years-old when Tommy was killed.

Tommy and my stepfather were out together one night. Tommy came back to our house with my stepfather. When it got late, Tommy decided to take off. Before heading home, he stopped at a bar. He was walking out of the bar when a guy mistook Tommy for someone else. My brother did not even know the man who shot him in half with a shotgun. Tommy was 21-years-old.

My stepfather was devastated. Just devastated. We all were. It was the first funeral I ever attended. I can still see Tommy lying in the casket. As a little boy, I had to come to an understanding of what "dead" meant.

A few years later, Mosetta got married and moved out of the house. Then it was just me, my mother, and my stepfather.

From then on, I was pretty much raised as an only child.

I still had plenty of family.

My mother had four sisters, and they all had a bunch of kids. We would have Thanksgiving dinner at my maternal grandmother's house with all the relatives. It would be a potluck with everyone bringing a dish. The little kids would sit at one table, and the bigger kids and the adults would sit at a different table. After dinner, we would have a drawing for who would give Christmas presents to whom, and everyone would pull out a name. Those Thanksgiving dinners were so much fun. I remember them like it was yesterday.

The neighborhood I grew up in in Ohio was called Cloverside. It was a middle-class, Black neighborhood. The residents were people like teachers, small business owners or government workers like my mom. Cloverside was on the other side of the Lee-Harvard area, which was White and wealthier.

I did not think about living in the poorer section, but I did know that the other side had bigger houses.

Cloverside was considered segregated. When Black people moved into the neighborhood, the Whites moved out. Cloverside was 99-percent Black. Any of the White kids who lived there were trapped because their families did not have any money. I think I had just one White kid on my street. Other than those few White kids, everyone else was Black.

It seemed normal at the time. That was just how it was, and I never really worried about it. My elementary school was all Black except for one White girl. I never had any White friends until I went to high school at Gilmour Academy. In high school, I would bring some of my White friends down to my neighborhood to meet some of my Black friends so everyone would realize what I had learned: We were all the same.

Growing up, we did not have Black History Month. We did not even have Black History Day. The first time I ever missed school on purpose was when my mom said that we were having a "Civil Rights Day." We were trying to get just one day to honor Black people.

I never really got a sense about the Civil Rights movement until I got to college and learned more about it. I did not think about Civil Rights. I never had to interface with racism growing up, so it did not matter to me.

My mother had to face racism every day. My stepfather had to face it every day. It was not something people paid attention to like they do now, though. We did not have any Black Power marches or movements. We lived in our community and all took care of each other. My whole family was about the village. The village raised me. When something was going wrong, we would all huddle around each other and do what we had to do to make it work.

My mother and my aunties went to college and were educated. My grandmother went to The Normal School for Colored Girls, which is now known as University of the District of Columbia.

My mother always taught me to be who I was and not to worry about everyone else. She told me, "Be what you are, and who you are. You deserve to be who you are." I listened, and I was good to go.

My family expected all of the kids to speak right and act right.

When we would drive down the street, if I said, "There *goes* Jerry's house." My mother would say, "Where's Jerry's house *going*?" I would have to say, 'Oh, I get it, ma. There *is* Jerry's house."

My mother always made me articulate my words when I talked. It was not talking White vs. talking Black. It was just how we talked in my house.

When I began going to St. Henry's, a mostly White middle school, I used to talk one way with the Black kids and another way with the White kids.

"Man, you talk two languages," a Black friend once said to me.

"What are you talking about?" I asked. "I talk the same to everyone."

"No," he said, "you talk this way to us and that way to them."

And I guess I did. But I did it so seamlessly, I never noticed that it was happening.

It is funny because now, with all of my teeth missing due to diabetes, I cannot articulate words the way I want.

While I did not have White friends when I was younger, I was around White people a lot growing up. My mother was Catholic. The Catholic church that I went to with her was primarily White. My grandmother was Baptist. The church that I went to with her was mostly Black.

Religion and God have been a part of my life, all of my life. Since Day One.

My mother and stepfather raised me Catholic and my grandmother raised me Baptist. My birth-father was a Jehovah's witness, though I never participated in that religion.

Which Church was my favorite, Catholic or Baptist? Neither one. But I had to go to both churches. Every Sunday. Without fail.

Splitting time between the churches is one of the reasons I now identify as Nondenominational. Both religions believe in God. Everybody at both churches worships God. Everybody reads the same King James version of the Bible. My mother and stepfather were great people as Catholics. My grandmother and aunties were great women as Baptists. So, to me, the religions are very much the same.

One of my uncles was a pastor at the Baptist church where my grandmother and all my aunties went.

At the Baptist Church, I would get rambunctious and cut up all the time. My grandmother would pop me in the back of the head. When I settled down and stopped playing around, she would give me a piece of mint so I would be good.

My family was hard on my mother because she switched over and became Catholic. She had gotten a divorce from my father so she was not allowed to receive communion for a time. The Monsignor gave her a penance plan with things to do like go to church and read the Catechism. She did those things, and she was eventually able to receive communion.

I went through the Catholic sacraments growing up: Baptism; Confession; First Communion; and Confirmation.

I remember being at the Baptist church when my Aunt Ethel died. She used to call me "Chocolate Soldier" because I was the darkest person in my family.

It helped to have religion when dealing with tragedy.

Music was also a big part of my childhood. Everybody in my family played an instrument. Well, my stepfather did not play anything because he worked all the time. But the rest of us had to learn to play an instrument and sing. That was just the kind of family I came from.

My sister played the piano. I have big hands but short fingers, so I could never play the piano. I played the trumpet instead. I had private lessons and was in a band with some of my friends in high school. I used to play for my grandmother. I could also sing pretty well. I cannot remember words to songs, but I can hum a tune. I was not like Louis Armstrong, singing and playing the trumpet, but I thought I was pretty good.

Eventually, I played the trumpet enough that I got "trumpeter's wart" on my lip. Then, playing football in high school, I got my lip busted up. I really never played the trumpet again after that.

While I played music, my real love was always sports.

The neighborhood kids used to go out on the street and have races around the block. I was always the fastest kid in the neighborhood.

I would also play in "unorganized, organized" football games. We called ourselves the Cloverside VIPs. We did not have coaches. We would just gather on the local high school football field and play tackle football.

One of the kids who helped organize the Cloverside VIPs was my lifelong friend William P. Jones III. William was three years older than me. I was just a little guy, pushing toy cars around when we met. William took me under his wing and acted as a "trainer" of sorts throughout my childhood and even after I got to Notre Dame. He was not the kind of athlete I was, but he was a great trainer. He knew me from when I was a little kid until I was a big kid.

The Cloverside VIP games were rough. People got hurt. We did not have uniforms because we did not have the money for uniforms. We did not have pads because pads were for wimps. We just put on our shoes, and we went out and played football.

I would always play running back. I was the youngest kid on the team, but the other kids picked me to be the main running back because I was better than everyone else.

I would play linebacker when I had to play defense, but I liked running back much better. That was where I had the most fun. You either could not catch me, or I would run over you. I had some jukes, but mostly, I just outran everyone. For the rest of my life, I was always a running back.

Coming from Cleveland, I was of course a Jim Brown fan. I would eventually start wearing Number 44 because it was the number both Brown and running back Ernie Davis had worn while they played at Syracuse.

In 1961, Davis had become the first Black player to win the Heisman Trophy. He was drafted by the Washington Football Team with the No. 1 overall pick in the 1962 draft, then traded immediately to the Cleveland Browns. Davis was diagnosed with leukemia that same year, though, and died at 23-years-old without ever playing a professional football game.

My favorite football player was Dickie Post, a 5-9, 190-pound White running back on the San Diego Chargers. Post was small and slightly built like I was back then. At the time, I never thought

I would be closer to Jim Brown's size by the time I got to Notre Dame.

I played hockey too. My parents bought me skates and a hockey stick and a puck. I was not very good, though. I also played some baseball, and I had a basketball hoop in my backyard. Sometimes I would even throw horseshoes. You name a sport, and we were doing it around my neighborhood along with riding our bikes and playing with toy army soldiers.

My parents encouraged me to be out of the house. They wanted me to be around the neighborhood and not get into trouble. Some kids around the neighborhood got into trouble, including one of my good friends. But mostly, playing outside all day, my friends and I stayed out of trouble.

I saved my time getting into trouble for school.

I probably had what they now call attention deficit hyperactivity disorder (ADHD). I was always misbehaving. I was always bored. I did well enough to get by because I was smart. But I could not sit still. I still cannot sit still, actually. Back then, though, I was a hummingbird all the time. Just hyper.

I used to get swatted and hit and stuff back in the days when teachers could do that. And then they would send me up to the principal's office.

At one point, the school tested me to try to figure out what my problem was. The test showed that I actually was smart. The school put me into enrichment classes, which were more advanced. Being challenged a little more, I started doing better academically. The school eventually told my parents that the best thing for me would be to go to a place where I could get a lot of attention.

So, from sixth grade through eighth grade I went to St. Henry's, a mostly White, private Catholic School. I was really blessed to be able to go there. With the extra attention from teachers, I started doing much better in school.

At St. Henry's, I got great test scores and had interest from private high schools. The best of those high schools was Gilmour Academy, a Brothers of the Holy Cross Catholic High School.

Gilmour required an essay for acceptance. I wrote my essay on Dr. Daniel Hale Williams. My mother believed in teaching me about Black History, and Dr. Williams was one of her heroes.

Dr. Williams founded Provident Hospital, America's first non-segregated hospital, in 1891. He was also the first Black man to successfully perform open-heart surgery.

I wrote about how Dr. Williams had been instrumental in my background and my life. I said that Dr. Williams had shown me how much I could accomplish in my life.

With my test scores and my paper, Gilmour Academy offered me their "Interracial Scholarship."

CHAPTER 2

I can see it in my mind, but I cannot explain just how wonderful Gilmour Academy was. Going to that school was my favorite time in life. It was just a beautiful, beautiful place to grow up and go to high school.

Gilmour is located in Gates Mill, Ohio, which was a *long* way from where I lived. At least 30 or 40 miles. I would have to piece together busses to get there. I had to take a long public city bus ride into Cleveland, then catch another long school bus ride to Gilmour.

The travel time and waking up early in the morning to catch the busses was more than worth it.

Gilmour was not just one little high school building. It was a campus. The library was over here, the cafeteria was in an old mansion over there. There was a horticultural building. Gilmour had an early version of a computer that took up an entire room. There was an art barn.

I spent a lot of time in the art barn. The upstairs portion contained an exercise system that was very advanced for the time. It was a machine with pulleys and weights that allowed for a full body workout. I used to go there every day to lift on my lunch breaks. I was lifting weights in high school at a time before a lot of college or even professional athletes were lifting weights. Most of the guys that I played football with and against in college were not as strong as I was in high school.

Gilmour was one of the smaller schools in the state. The class sizes at Gilmour were very small. We had about 10 students per class. My whole graduating class had around 65 students, and that was the largest graduating class Gilmour had ever had at the time.

It felt like we always had one-on-one time with the teachers.

The high-touch environment was perfect for me. I started doing very well academically. I was still a little wild, but the teachers would slow me down and give me a whole bunch of stuff to do.

The academic challenges at Gilmour were ridiculous. We had high-level science classes with chemistry and biology and rigorous math classes with algebra and calculus. I took Latin instead of French, and I learned the derivatives of different words. One of our English teachers was able to sit around and perfectly quote the Shakespeare plays we were reading. Gilmour had all of the students take the PSATs as sophomores. We would then take the SATs as juniors and then take the SATs again as seniors to improve our scores.

Gilmour made me realize that I really liked school. I liked learning. I was having fun using my brain. It was a challenge, but that challenge allowed me to see how smart I could become.

Gilmour was a Catholic school, so we had religion classes. Religion was not forced on you, but it was part of the deal of going to Gilmour. I believe receiving a Catholic education was the best thing that ever happened to me.

After getting a rare bad grade in a class at Gilmour, my mother made me go to summer school. I retook the class at John F. Kennedy High, a public high school in Cleveland. There were times when I felt like I was the dumbest person in class at Gilmour. In summer school, though, I was by far the smartest kid in the class, and I easily got an A.

My senior year at Gilmour, I had to do a year-end project that required me to do some research at John Adams High. It was supposed to be one of the best public schools in my area. John Adams High School had really old books. The chemistry lab had carvings on the tables. It was just shocking compared to how nice Gilmour was.

What truly made Gilmour Academy so special was the friends I made there. My friends and I called ourselves the Gilmour Men. I always say that before I became a Notre Dame Man, I was a Gilmour Man. The reason I became who I was at Notre Dame was because I went to Gilmour. Those kids—they are all grown men like me now—but those guys had an enormous impact upon my life. I would not have been able to face the hard things I went through at Notre Dame, and later in life, if I had not become a Gilmour Man.

I think of the Gilmour Men often.

Dave Janasek and Joe Ruglovsky were fullbacks who shared the backfield with me. Scott Carson was our wingback.

Gilmour's quarterbacks were John Schenkelberg who was one of my best friends when I was in high school, and Art Rooney who is now the owner of the Pittsburgh Steelers.

Our linemen included Bob Hillis and Mike Elliott who became a lawyer and still helps me out a lot. Bill Velotta played tight end and always blocked down on my outside runs.

Mike Svoboda and Frank Piraino anchored Gilmour's defense.

John Eby was the fastest 20-yard guy you will ever meet and taught me how to get a fast start on the track. Bob Wright was always in the art barn with me.

There was Tony Panzica who is a really good guy, and Tim Coleman, whose uncle had created the Interracial Scholarship Foundation, allowing me to attend Gilmour.

Fred Kuglin visited me all the time and looked after me while we were both living in Texas. Bob Zhun helps us all stay in touch and keeps us together today.

Those guys really did have such a big impact on my life, and they continue to have an impact on my life now. We have a reunion almost every year. In November, a bunch of us will go down to Florida to reconnect on a beach holiday.

The Gilmour Men are my lifelong buddies.

Gilmour was mostly White. Being a different race than my classmates never bothered me. To be honest, I did not really think about it. My friends at Gilmour and I did not have any hangups about race at all. My Black friends from my neighborhood used to tease me and tell me that our local high school would have won the football state championship with me as their running back. Really, though, they thought it was cool that I was going to a place like Gilmour Academy.

I did experience some racism from opposing teams during football games.

When Gilmour played a Black team, sometimes some of the Black kids would say things like, "What're you doing over there, brother?"

When Gilmour played a White team, sometimes some of the White kids, or the White fans would call me racist names.

Those were the times of the day.

Of course, being called racial epithets hurt my feelings. But, my teammates at Gilmour, the people I cared about, they did not call me anything bad, and they were not mean to me. That is what was really important to me.

I was not supposed to play sports at all at Gilmour. My mother did not like sports whatsoever. She wanted me to go to school for one reason and one reason only: Academics.

Then, in my freshman gym class, I ran a barefoot, 11-something-second 100-yard-dash. Our gym teacher, Vern Weber was also the track coach and football coach. He begged my mother to let me run track and play football.

"No," my mother said. "He's there for academics."

Mr. Weber kept begging and eventually, that spring, my mother allowed me to run track.

Being able to play sports actually helped me do even better in school. I knew I had to do well academically for my mother to let me participate. Athletics helped ground me as a student.

Track was a huge thing in Ohio at the time. I fell in love with it. Track is an individual sport. You win or lose based on your own merits. You could prove how good you were by how hard you worked. I worked very hard, and I became very good.

I used to be faster than everyone in my neighborhood. I just looked at it like the neighborhood got bigger. All of a sudden, I was in a state neighborhood vs. a little neighborhood.

Frank Brandt became Gilmour's track coach my junior and senior seasons. Mr. Brandt was a math teacher and he did everything mathematically. He would calculate how to do the workouts to get us into perfect shape. He even had our starting blocks measured to be exactly the right fit for each sprinter. Mr. Brandt was just a fantastic coach as well as a great person. All I had to do was follow what he told me to do.

As a freshman, I set the school record in the 100-yard-dash. I also ran the 220-yard-dash (now called the 200 meters), and threw the shotput.

I eventually became fast enough that I was invited to run with a college club called the Ohio Striders in the summer. Those guys were just phenomenally fast, and they made me even faster.

As a junior, I won the Ohio State Championship in both the 100-yard-dash and 220-yard-dash. I also got to go to the Junior Olympics in Kentucky where I took third place in the 100-yard-dash.

As a senior, Mr. Brandt moved me up to the 440-yard-dash (now called the 400-meters). During the regular season, I just ran the 440, the relays and threw the shotput.

"You already know you can win the 100 and the 220, so that's not a big deal," Mr. Brandt said. "We need you to run for the team."

I wound up setting the school record in the shotput. Using the glide-and-turn method, I threw the 12-pound shot nearly 50-feet.

I was not as good at the 440 as I was at the shorter sprints, but I still got my time down to 48.6 seconds and won the Ohio State Championship. The 440 made me stronger and even faster for the shorter sprints. I defended my state championships, running the 100-yard-dash in 9.4 seconds and the 220-yard-dash in 21.7 seconds. Those three victories gave Gilmour enough points to win the state championship. At the time, I was the only high school athlete to ever score enough points to singlehandedly win a track state championship for the team.

My three State Championship wins as a senior made me an unprecedented five-time state champion in the sprints.

My mother was even more against me playing football than she had been against me running track. On top of football taking my focus away from academics, my mother was certain that I would hurt my lip and not be able to play the trumpet.

Mr. Weber kept begging my mother and begging her some more. Finally, by the time I was a sophomore, Mr. Weber broke my mother down.

"If he's going to play for you, you have to make sure his grades are taken care of, or he can't play," My mother said. "If his grades go down, or he gets hurt, or anything happens to him, he can't play. Period."

Mr. Weber promised my mother he would look after me. So, as a sophomore, I played my first year of organized football.

I did eventually ruin my lip for playing the trumpet, but other than that, I never got hurt in high school. My mother even came to a couple of football games and track meets.

I played on the junior varsity football team as a sophomore and just had a blast. I did not like getting hit, to be honest, but I eventually got used to it. I was running all over the place and scoring a whole lot of touchdowns.

At Gilmour, if you participated in sports you had to play a sport each season. So, as a sophomore I wrestled in the winter. Wrestling was OK, but I was never in love with it. I weighed about 154-pounds, but had to wrestle up at 165-pounds.

By my junior year, my mother said that I could not do sports year-round. The school allowed me to give up wrestling. I was not disappointed at all to be able to just play football and run track.

My junior year, I was the starting varsity running back on our undefeated team. Our team had about 10 plays. One of my backfield mates at Gilmour was Dave Janasek, a fullback who would go on to play college ball at Pittsburgh. People used to call us "Mr. Inside" and "Mr. Outside." I was "Mr. Outside," of course. Why go between the tackles when you could go outside where no one can catch you?

I was definitely not the kind of player who caught balls out of the backfield. I hated catching passes. You had to put your arms up and wait for someone to blast you. It is stupid and crazy! Fortunately, I did not really have to catch too many passes in high school, nor later at Notre Dame.

By the time I was a senior, I had grown a lot and put on a lot of muscle from lifting weights in the art barn. My senior year, the team lost just one game. I had over 2,000-yards rushing and was named an All American by just about every national ranking.

I liked track better than I liked football. There was no money to be made in track at the time. If you wanted to make money, you had to play football. The chance to get paid was the biggest reason why I liked football. I did not come from a rich family, and I wanted to make money for my family.

I may have grown up playing sports, but I did not know much about the world of college recruiting.

I learned quickly.

On top of being talented on the football field, I was going to a world-class prep school, and I had high SAT scores.

I hate to say it like this, but there was not a college in the country that did not recruit me.

With all of the Civil Rights craziness going on in the south, my mother shut down southern schools like Alabama right away.

It is interesting to look back and realize that I only had a vague sense of what was happening to Black people in the south at the time. My mother and stepfather kept me sheltered from a lot of stuff. That was their job. They did it extremely well. Now, I realize how good of a decision it was to not go to college in the south. I also realize how lucky I was as a Black person to be born and raised in the north.

I was recruited heavily by Big 10 schools like Michigan, Michigan State and Ohio State.

Famous Ohio State coach Woody Hayes came to my house and sat in the living room with my family.

"Mrs. Moon," Woody Hayes said, "I'll be just like your son's grandfather."

My mother scoffed and said, "His grandfather has been dead since before he was born."

My mother definitely, definitely, definitely did not care for Woody Hayes and what he had to say.

I gave Nebraska a lot of consideration. Looking back, going to Nebraska could have been interesting as I would have competed for the starting running back position against future Heisman Trophy winner Johnny Rodgers.

A couple of guys from my neighborhood went to school at Michigan and they lobbied for me to go there. At the time, I thought that I wanted to eventually go to law school. The Michigan recruiter told me, "You go here, we can guarantee that you can go to law school afterward."

I spent my senior year visiting a new college every week. I would go anywhere I could go and eat all the dinners I could eat and talk to all the coaches I could talk to. It was a lot of fun.

Then, Notre Dame assistant Coach Mike Stock came to recruit me.

I was on the radar of the Irish coaching staff because both Notre Dame and Gilmour Academy were Brothers of the Holy Cross Catholic schools. One of the Gilmour priests had taken my game film up to Notre Dame.

Once I had interest from Notre Dame, the recruiting process was over for my mother.

"Notre Dame is recruiting you," my mother said. "You aren't going anywhere else."

To be honest, I was pretty relaxed about where I went to school as long as I could get a good education and play football.

When my mother said, "The best place for you is Notre Dame," I trusted her.

I accepted the scholarship offer from the Fighting Irish and began my journey toward becoming a Notre Dame Man.

CHAPTER 3

College was my first experience ever truly being away from my home and my family. It was scary. All of a sudden, my parents left me in South Bend, Indiana. And there I was.

As football players, we had to be at Notre Dame before the rest of the incoming freshman for summer football practice. I was pretty much alone in the Cavanaugh Hall Dormitory. I had no roommate, and it did not seem like there was anyone else around.

The first person I met was Dwight Clay as his parents were dropping him off. Dwight was a point guard on the Notre Dame basketball team from Pittsburgh. Dwight would go on to make the game-winning shot that ended UCLA's 88-game win streak in 1974.

The first few days at Notre Dame were really hard. With no friends or support system, I used to call my parents all the time.

I told them that I wanted to come home.

"Well, Eric," my father said, "you've got Vietnam, or you've got going out and getting a job, or you've got college and football."

Neither getting a job, nor going to Vietnam sounded great, so I knew I was going to have to stay in school.

I was calling my parents well before unlimited cellphone plans. My parents finally told me that the long-distance phone calls cost too much, and I had to stop calling so often.

I had a record player that I listened to all the time. I lost count of how many times I played albums by the Chi-Lites and by the Spinners, my two favorite groups.

I could not do a lot around South Bend because I was broke and had no money.

I ate at the cafeteria for every meal. I know some of my

teammates hated the food at Notre Dame, but I thought it was pretty good. You would get as much as you wanted during the meals, which I loved. And then, we had extra food at dinner time with the team at Training Table.

I eventually got to know some of the guys on the football team and became good friends with them, including Al Samuel and Wayne Bullock.

What really turned my experience at Notre Dame around was a man named Ernie Rice. He was a security guard at Notre Dame.

One day, it could not have been more than a few weeks after I arrived in South Bend, I was wandering around campus. I was lonely. I happened to start talking to the security guard at the Notre Dame front gate.

Mr. Rice told me that he was a retired detective who had worked for the South Bend Police Department. He said that he had played football in South Bend in his youth, but that he was not allowed to go to Notre Dame because there was a lot of racial tension at the time.

Mr. Rice changed my life.

I eventually introduced Mr. Rice to Al and Wayne, and he cared about those guys too. Mr. Rice really took the Black players under his wing. He recognized that we were all feeling lonely and out of place in our own ways at Notre Dame.

My friends and I would go over to Mr. Rice's house to have dinner with him and his wife. At one time, I surely must have been told Mrs. Rice's first name. But I always just called her Mrs. Rice, and that is the only name I can remember for her. When Mrs. Rice died my senior year at Notre Dame, I was one of her pallbearers.

After we ate dinner with Mr. and Mrs. Rice, we would go down to their basement and watch TV. It felt just like we were at home. We were over at the Rice house all the time. It was such a good thing for us.

In those early days, just after I met Mr. Rice and was still feeling homesick, he told me, "You're not here at Notre Dame just for yourself. You're here for the community. So do your best all the time, and stop crying."

I will always remember that. I was still feeling anxious, but I started doing my best, and started to remember why I was at Notre Dame and that the community was 100-percent behind us all the time.

Mr. Rice was really like a father to me. Anytime I messed up, he was always on my case, making sure that I did right. I liked that.

At the time, I did not think about how lucky I was to have met Mr. Rice. I was just happy to have someone. All of a sudden, he was there and then we got close.

With Mr. Rice, I had the comfort on the domestic side of my life. Everything was complete and perfect, and I was happy.

It took a few months, but with new friends and adults looking out for me, I got over my homesickness, and my attitude changed.

Having that support system was especially important to me as one of the few Black people at Notre Dame in the early 1970s.

At the time, there were only a handful of Black players on the football team. There were some other Black kids at the school, but not too many. I was in Cavanaugh Hall. Most of the other Black people were in Alumni Hall, Notre Dame's primarily Black dorm. It was a small, small world for the Black students at Notre Dame.

The student body at Notre Dame was from all parts of the country. They were a lot different than the kids with whom I had been raised. They were not used to me, and I was not used to them.

Some of them were racist in their own way. Those kids used to call me a, "jock." I did not understand what that meant. Eventually, I figured out they were calling me a, "jockstrap." They thought that I only got into Notre Dame to play football. That was the only way they could see how a Black man like me would be at Notre Dame. I grew to loathe the term, "jock."

When people called me a "jock," I would fire back that I was at Notre Dame because I was smart, just like they were. I had learned how to face racism like that. I faced it the right way. My mother's way.

A lot of other students were enamored with me because I was on the football team. Everybody knew who the football players were. It was kind of cool, but I would get embarrassed most of the time.

I was just a football player.

With rare exceptions, among the students, the players on the football team were the only family I ever had at Notre Dame.

CHAPTER 4

Summer practices at Notre Dame are legendary for the brutal heat. South Bend is hot and humid in the summer. Wearing pads and a helmet, practices could be unbearable. Especially during double practices. I also played at a time when the prevailing theory was that denying players water during practice would help toughen us up.

I did OK in the summer practices, though. I may have been born in September, but September, 1953 was unseasonably warm in Cleveland, and I never had a problem with the heat. I would just sweat and do what I had to do.

Actually, the winter practices were much worse. I did not wear gloves because that was for wimps. So, I would get my hands covered in snow and they would get all wet. I think the tips of my fingers might still be frostbitten from those winter practices.

Regardless of the season, the practices Coach Parseghian organized were always tough. Throughout my time at Notre Dame, I spent the week waiting for games on Saturday so I could have an "easy" day. Ara used to run us to death, doing the monkey drill and the serpent drill and jumping jacks and everything else. Everyone on the team was in great shape.

That was perfect for me because I was unable to lift as often in college as I had been able to in high school.

I used to lift weights all the time at the art barn at Gilmour. At Notre Dame, I did not actually know where the weightroom was! On top of practice, though, I would still do a lot of pushups and sit ups. My stomach was so strong at that time that you could punch me in the gut, and I would not even feel it.

From my first practice at Notre Dame, I felt like I had a lot of friends. There were of course some guys on the team who liked to pick on me and thought that was fun. I never liked being teased, so I just ignored it. I was at Notre Dame to play football, run track and get my education. I never bothered with all the other B.S..

In the early 1970s, freshmen were not allowed to play on the varsity. It wound up making for an easy transition into playing college football.

As a freshman, my only goal was to be the starting running back. I wanted to be the best on the team. I wound up as No. 1 on the depth chart, so I figured I was playing pretty well.

I thought freshman football was much the same as high school football. Guys hit harder, of course, but that was to be expected. I was still the fastest guy on the field.

The highlight of the year for the freshman team was when we went to Mexico City to play against the Mexico Football All Stars.

In 1967 I had gone with my family to the World's Fair in Montreal, Canada (Expo 67), but other than that, I had never been out of the country.

Going to Mexico City with the team was so much fun. We were just a bunch of 17-year-old and 18-year-old babies. It was the first time I had ever been at a hotel by myself. That was probably true for most of the players. We were all just laughing and having fun.

Our Notre Dame team managers, Mike Busick and Mark Dwyer, kept us in line. The biggest order the coaches gave us on the trip was not to drink the water.

One might call the game against the Mexico Football All Stars a borderline route. Notre Dame won 81-0.

I remember taking a handoff, breaking through the line of scrimmage and then going untouched, sprinting 97-yards for a touchdown. Mexico City has an elevation of 7,349-feet, so it is not surprising that when I got to the sideline, I promptly passed out. A full sprint for 97-yards in full pads, in the thin air, was no joke.

The Notre Dame Freshman team played other games that year against other Freshman teams like Michigan State and Tennessee. In essence, those games were glorified scrimmages. They were preparing us for the real games the following season.

When the freshman season ended, I felt that I had accomplished everything I needed to accomplish to be the starting varsity running back the next year.

On Saturdays during the fall, the freshman team would sit in the stands at Notre Dame Stadium and watch the real Irish football games.

We were all just waiting for our time.

CHAPTER 5

When I went to Notre Dame, my plan was to run track as well as play football. Even though I knew football was where I could make money, track was still my true love.

After the freshmen football season ended, I joined the track team for the indoor season.

Alex Wilson was the Notre Dame track coach at the time. Wilson was a former Notre Dame runner who went to the 1928 and 1932 Olympics, representing Canada. In 1928, he won a bronze medal in the 4X400 meter relay. In 1932, he took silver in the 800 meters, bronze in the 400 meters and bronze in the 4X400 meter relay. Coach Wilson was a great coach and a great guy.

As the season began, Coach Wilson asked me to run the 600-meters. I told him he was crazy. He convinced me to run some 300-meter races, but my best event indoors was the 60-meters. I remember winning most of my races.

The indoor season was great, highlighted by a trip to the Penn Relays, one of the world's most historic track meets.

When outdoor track season started, I went down with the team to a meet at Middle Tennessee State. During the 100-yard-dash, I exploded out of the blocks and accelerated down the track. As I was hitting my stride, I felt my hamstring give out.

Back in South Bend, Coach Parseghian heard about my pulled hamstring. When the track team returned from Tennessee, he called me into his office.

"Eric, are you here to play football or run track?" Ara asked.

"I'm here to play football," I said.

"Well," Ara said, "then why are you running track and getting hurt?"

I did not have a good answer for that.

"That's it then," Ara said. "That was the end of your track career. You're finished."

I was sad because I really did love track, and I had hopes of running in the Olympics one day. It was not to be, though. I knew football was the priority, so that is what I focused on.

CHAPTER 6

A lot of students find it difficult to transition from high school to college. Gilmour Academy was not a run-of-the-mill high school, though. With how strenuous Gilmour was academically, my freshman year at Notre Dame was a breeze. Everything I did as a freshman was basically what I had learned at Gilmour. That says more about Gilmour than it does about Notre Dame. Gilmour was just very, very advanced and did an incredible job of preparing me for college.

My mother was really mad because she was worried that my education was suffering. She went ballistic when she found out that my academic advisor had put me in remedial math. My mother called the advisor's office and let them have it.

"No, no, no, no, no," my mother said. "That boy took calculus in high school. What are you talking about remedial math? He went to private school. No, no, no, no, no."

And the next thing I knew, I was out of remedial math.

My mother did not ask me about football or track, but she always wanted to know about school. I found ways to ease her mind.

"What are you doing tonight?" my mother would ask when she called the dorm to talk with me.

"I'm going to The Library, mamma," I would say.

This conversation was repeated often. And I *was* going to The Library. I just did not tell my mother that The Library was the name of a college bar next to our campus.

My friends and I did drink. But everybody drinks a lot at college. My friends and I would stick to beer, though. For a young man working out all day, going to football practice and running countless stadium steps, it was impossible to put on any beer weight.

As a Catholic, I was required to go to mass and take religion classes my freshman year. I was really still a kid, though, and church was still boring.

I stopped going to mass weekly after my freshman year except during football season when the team had to attend mass before games. I should have gone to church more often. I thought I was *the* Eric Penick, though. I was happy-go-lucky, but I did not go to church and do the things my mother had told me to do.

All of the Notre Dame priests were into football. Notre Dame is Notre Dame. Catholicism and Irish football go hand-in-hand in South Bend.

Some of the professors were really into football as well. Most of the time they were professional about it, though. While they knew that you played football, they would not make a big deal about you. When you were in class, you were there to learn. You had to make your grades so that you could keep playing football. I really did like that.

My freshman year may have been easy, but sophomore year was very tough. By the time I was a sophomore, the professors got down to it.

I learned that I was going to have to declare a major. I never realized I would have to do that. At the time, I thought I was just going to go to college the way I had gone to high school.

My dream was to play football professionally. Outside of that, though, I was convinced that I wanted to become a lawyer. There was no such thing as a pre-law bachelor's degree at Notre Dame, though.

Notre Dame tight end and future College and NFL Hall of Famer Dave Casper told me I would like economics and that I should major in it. I knew Dave was an Irish team captain, and I knew that he was really smart. So, I listened to him and became an economics major.

At first, I had my doubts about Dave's advice because I did not understand what was going on in the classes I was taking. Dave reassured me that I would not have any problems, though. He was right. Once I understood what was going on, I thought economics was fun and I began enjoying it.

Economics really is the basis for all of business. I liked it so much that for a time I actually considered becoming an economics professor.

After my freshman year, school was definitely challenging, but I put in the work over my sophomore, junior and senior years, going to school year-round. I would eventually walk out of Notre Dame with my bachelor's degree and a worldclass education.

CHAPTER 7

I had mixed emotions about becoming Notre Dame's starting running back in 1972.

On one hand, I had a great year on the Irish Freshman team. I was 5-11, 210-pounds and lightning fast. I believed I deserved to be Notre Dame's starting running back. On the other hand, I moved into the No. 1 slot on the depth chart after the 1971 starter was suspended from the team. As excited as I was about getting to start, the previous starter was a Black running back from Ohio just like me, and I felt bad at the same time.

In 1972, our offense was a Power-I scheme with two tailbacks split on either side of the quarterback. The way it worked out, the player on the right side was always Black and the player the left side was always White. We never, ever lined up with a White right half back or a Black left half back.

My sophomore year, I was the starting right tailback. It wound up working out pretty well for me once I got the racial aspect of it out of my head.

I joined a veteran backfield that included Darryll Dewan, Andy Huff and John Cieszkowski. Two years earlier, Cieszkowski had run roughshod over the No. 1 ranked Texas Longhorns in the 1970 Cotton Bowl. Notre Dame had snapped the Longhorns 30-game win streak, making Texas Coach Darrell Royal so frustrated that he had to comment, "We're not even slowing him (Cieszkowski) down."

Notre Dame was stacked at quarterback in 1972 with veterans Cliff Brown, Pat Steenberge, Jim Bulger, Tom Creevey and Bill Etter competing for the starting role against sophomore QBs, Tom Clements and Frank Allocco. As the season began, Clements was named our starter.

I had great lineman with players blocking for me like senior captain John Dampeer, and center Dave Drew. I also got great blocks throughout the season by Mike Creaney who had been Joe Theismann's favorite tight end.

The 1972 team had the Townsend brothers, Mike playing safety and Willie playing receiver. Our receiving corps also utilized Bob Washington and Jim Roolf, who made an array of circus catches throughout the season.

Our defense was led by linebackers Jim O'Malley, Tim Sullivan and Jim Musuraca. The defense also featured Greg Marx: Ken Schlezes; Tom Freistroffer; Jeff Hein; Pat McGraw; Terry Garner; John Mariani; and Dan O'Toole.

We had star players on special teams with Mike Naughton and Jim Zloch.

My first real college football game was on the road against Northwestern. We blew the Wildcats off the field 37-0.

I scored my first collegiate touchdown against Northwestern, taking a handoff nine-yards into the end zone on the opening series of the second half.

A week later, I played at Notre Dame Stadium for the first time in a matchup against Purdue. In my introduction to the fans in South Bend, I ran for 133-yards on 12 carries (11.1-yards-per-carry), scored a 14-yard touchdown, and the Irish won 35-14.

At Gilmour, there were at most a couple of hundred fans at our football games, typically friends and relatives. Now, I was playing before tens of thousands of people. That did not faze me. I knew I could play football, and I knew I could run the ball. Playing before so many people did not bother me anymore than playing before so few people had bothered me. When I was in a game, I was not paying attention to the crowd, or anything else in the world. I was just trying to do the things that I needed to do on the field.

The way I always played football was that I would dream about the game the night before. And then I went out, and I played it on Gameday. I did not see anybody in the stands. I just played football. I liked being on the field. Whether the Irish were at home or on the road, it was just me playing in a football game.

There were challenges in my first year playing real college football.

To start with, I did not really know any of our plays.

Gilmour had about 10 plays, and I was so much faster than everyone else on the field that I did not have to worry about the two-hole or the three-hole or where I was *supposed* to run the ball. I just got the ball and outran everyone.

At Notre Dame, we had a whole notebook full of plays. I did not know any of them. Our quarterback, sophomore Tom Clements, used to tell me, "Eric, you're going to get the ball. Go here." Or, "Eric, you're going to get the ball. Go there." Tom could not even tell me what hole in the line of scrimmage to go through because I did not know any of the hole numbers.

I listened to Tom and just cruised on talent and desire. I may not have known the plays, but I always wanted to be the best player on the field every Saturday.

Another challenge I had as a sophomore was that I had a really hard time holding onto the football.

I had a bad habit of carrying the ball too low. In track, you swing your arms as fast as you can when you sprint. As a tailback, I did the same. That worked at Gilmore when I was running so fast that I was rarely touched. In college, I was getting hit a lot more, and I was getting hit a lot harder. A lot of fumbles my sophomore year did not happen on hard tackles, though. I would just be running, holding the ball low and not really paying attention to who was going to hit me.

One of my clearest memories of the 1972 season was a home game against Texas Christian University on October 28. I broke away and was running down the field with a clear path to the endzone. I was holding the ball so low that my knee hit my arm. No joke, I kicked the ball out of my own hand.

The Irish beat TCU 21-0, and I finished with 158-yards on 16 carries (9.9-yards-per-carry), and scored a touchdown. I fumbled twice, though, and that play where I kicked the ball out of my own hand just embarrassed the hell out of me.

The Irish lost three games in 1972. The first was a 30-26 home loss against Missouri. The second loss was against USC. The Trojans blew us out, 45-23 in Los Angeles.

The Trojans had a great defense that year and held me to just 24-yards on the ground.

That game really disgusted me. I hated USC with a passion. And I really could not stand USC running back Anthony Davis.

Davis had an extraordinary game against Notre Dame that day, scoring six touchdowns. He ran back two kickoffs for scores (97-yards on the opening kickoff and another TD return for 96-yards). He rushed for 99-yards on 22 carries (4.5-yards-per-carry) and scored four touchdowns on runs of one-yard, five-yards, four-yards, and eight-yards.

It was not Davis scoring touchdowns that really upset me. It was how he acted after he scored. Davis was a "hotdog" before "hotdogs" were cool. I still do not think "hotdogs" are cool. I can remember Davis scoring against the Irish defense and sliding across the field on his knees. That was the first time I had ever seen someone act like that on the football field. To me, there are 11 guys on the field, and 10 guys help a running back score a touchdown. I have no idea why a running back would need to dance around and do stupid stuff after scoring.

After watching Davis sliding across the field on his knees, I turned to the closest guy to me on the sideline and said, "I'm never going to do that when we score a touchdown. This is Notre Dame."

There were a lot of highlights from my sophomore season as well.

In a 16-0 win at Michigan State, I had a memorable 26-yard run, on which I broke several tackles. The turf in East Lansing was really funky at the time, and after the game, my arms were all bruised and cut up. The Spartans were very tough. They were keying on me and trying to beat me up. It was a really fun game.

The next week against Pittsburgh, I got to play against my former Gilmour teammate, Dave Janasek, "Mr. Inside," who was Pittsburgh's fullback.

I helped Notre Dame to a 42-16 win over Pitt with a two-yard TD run.

I also got to play against the Academy schools for the first time. In back-to-back weeks, we beat Navy 42-23 and Air Force 21-7.

The military schools always played hard and they never gave up. That was the only thing I did not like about playing against them. They never stopped. You would knock them down, they would come back up. You would knock them down, they would come back up. They were tenacious. Very tenacious. The players were small, though. And I always knew I would pick up yards against them.

Against Navy, I ran for 101-yards on 11 carries (9.2-yards-per-carry) and scored a touchdown. Against Air Force, I gained 82-yards on 12 carries (6.8-yards-per-carry).

In the early 1970s, official college football stats only accounted for the regular season, not bowl games. I finished the 1972 regular season as the Irish's top rusher, gaining 727-yards on 124 carries (5.9-yards-per-carry) and scoring five touchdowns. I also caught two passes for nine-yards. I was elated when the coaches told me that my 727-yards on the ground was the second most rushing yards in school history at the time.

It was a good year, other than the fumbles. If I had not fumbled so many times as a sophomore, I might have broken 1,000-yards.

I gained an additional 48-yards in the Orange Bowl against Nebraska. I could have gained more if I had been able to play the whole game.

CHAPTER 8

I was really excited to play in the Orange Bowl. Nebraska had been one of my top choices for college, and I wanted to see how I could play against them.

The night before the game, there was a big parade on the streets of Miami. I snuck out of my room with a teammate and we went to watch. We were not drinking or doing anything bad. We were just out there having fun and watching the parade. Then, we joined the parade and started marching. And then, someone let us get onto one of the parade floats. I was laughing and tossing balls out to the crowd and just acting silly.

All of a sudden, the float rolled passed none other than Ara Parseghian.

Later that night, Ara was waiting for me in the hotel lobby. He was *really* mad. I knew I had screwed up and that I was in big trouble.

"Get upstairs," Ara barked. That was about all I can remember him saying.

When I looked at the depth chart the next day, I was nowhere to be found.

Ara made me stand next to him and watch the whole first half on the sidelines.

"Stand next to me, Penick, and don't move," Ara said.

Ara finally let me into the game in the second half. By that time, the Irish were already trailing 20-0. I gained 48-yards on eight carries (6-yards-per-carry), including a long run of 21-yards. I played OK. But it was like my whole mojo was gone.

Nebraska Heisman Trophy winner Johnny Rodgers had a much better day than I did. Rodgers led the Cornhuskers to a 40-6 win with an historic performance. He rushed for 81-yards and three touchdowns on 15 carries (5.4-yards-per-carry), caught three passes for 71-yards and one touchdown, and even threw a 52-yard touchdown pass.

It was either the day of the game, or the next day that I had to tell my mother what had happened and why I had not played until the second half. It was really embarrassing. But it was a good lesson to not fool around and to make sure I did what I needed to do before a game.

With the loss to Nebraska, Notre Dame finished the season 8-3 and was ranked as the No. 14 team in the nation by the Associated Press.

It was a solid year for the Irish and for me personally.

I went into the offseason knowing I had to improve a lot if I wanted to reach my personal goals and help the team have a better season the next year.

CHAPTER 9

After my freshman year at Notre Dame, I spent the summer in Cleveland working a construction job knocking down and then reinforcing walls in a school cafeteria. It was a decent job as far as getting me in shape, but I absolutely hated it. From that point on, I spent my summers in South Bend, taking summer school classes. That allowed me to graduate easily and also focus on preparing for the next football season.

During the summer between my sophomore and junior seasons, one of my biggest focuses was not fumbling so darn much.

I spent the whole summer walking around campus with a football in my hands. People would sneak up on me and try to hit the ball out of my hand. They thought it was funny, and it was funny. I was just walking around campus holding a football like an idiot. I never felt embarrassed about it. It was just what I had to do. I learned very quickly how to hold onto the ball tightly and by the end of the summer, no one could get the ball out of my hands. Those were really good times.

I have vivid memories of doing the famous run around St. Mary's Lake. I ran that 2.2 mile loop all summer and was in great shape by fall camp.

I will not lie and say that I studied the playbook, but by the time my junior season began, I had run the plays so many times, repetition, repetition, repetition, that I knew the system by heart.

I was ready for what would be an historic 1973 Notre Dame football season.

CHAPTER 10

Notre Dame did not admit women until the fall of 1972. It did not really seem strange to me, though, since Gilmour Academy was an all-boys school.

Going to an all-boys high school presented me with a unique opportunity. I was famous. Well, I was high school famous. I also had a lot of "game" as a young man. I wound up with four girlfriends who went to four different schools. There was Karen, Robin, Sharon and Acquanetta. The girls went to John Adams High, John F. Kennedy High, Hathaway Brown High, and Glenville High, respectively.

With three of those girls, once I graduated high school and went to Notre Dame, it was what it was. The relationships ended. But even after I got to Notre Dame, I remembered the girl from Glenville High, Acquanetta. She was the most special of all of them.

I called her A.C. because that was a lot easier than calling her Acquanetta. She was a year younger than me. I met her through her uncle. He was a policeman who lived on my street.

I kept thinking about A.C. while I was at Notre Dame. I saw her whenever I was back in Cleveland. I was madly in love with her. I eventually got tired of going back and forth to Cleveland to see her. I wanted her with me in South Bend.

My mother told me to wait, but I just could not do it. I proposed to A.C.. The summer between my sophomore and junior year, we got married. I was 19-years-old. A.C. was 18-years-old.

A.C. and I got married in Birmingham, Alabama, where she was born. The ceremony was at an all-Black church where Dr. Martin Luther King Jr. had once spoken.

Notre Dame assistant coach George Kelly gave me a candle symbolizing marital happiness as a wedding present. Coach Parseghian even came down to Alabama for the ceremony.

A.C. enrolled at Holy Cross College, which is practically next door to Notre Dame. We moved into an off-campus apartment together. One of our friends owned an R.V. company. He was able to get us all the furniture we needed. The furniture was old and raggedy, but it was sturdy.

I did not feel like I missed out on anything by getting married so young. I had dated a lot before I got to college. By the time A.C. and I got married, I was glad to be slowing myself down.

After I got hurt, I got mean and everything with A.C. imploded. That came later, though. When we first got married, it was like I was living under a clear blue sky whenever I was with A.C.. When I was lonely, I had someone to be with me. When I got sick, someone was there to take care of me. It made a big difference.

A.C. was right beside me my junior season as the Irish marched toward the 1973 National Championship.

CHAPTER 11

When I first got to Notre Dame and looked around at the guys we had on the team, I thought winning the National Championship would be a foregone conclusion.

I saw incredible talent with guys like future consensus All American Mike Fanning; Greg Collins; Ed Bauer; Steve Quehl; Tom Fine; Tim Miller; Tom Bake; Chuck Kelly; Jim Chauncey; Andy Rohan; and Bill Arment.

Talent-wise, the players on our team were good, even great. There was also a burning desire to win inside every man.

My junior year in 1973, our team was phenomenally talented. I was sure we could win the National Championship that year. Because Notre Dame does not play in a conference, there was no conference championship to try to win. That meant that the only big carrot for us was the National Championship. That was what I focused on. I had my own individual desires, of course. I wanted to rush for 1,000-yards and be an All American. But my major goal was for the team to be National Champs.

1973 was just a magical season for the Irish. We bookended the regular season with a 44-0 win against Northwestern and a 44-0 win against Miami. Of course, my jersey number was 44.

Ara Parseghian had coached at Northwestern from 1956-1963. We did not try to run up the score against the Wildcats. Coach Parseghian never tried to run up the score against anyone, actually. Certainly not the way teams do today. Against Northwestern, we got the second and even the third team into the game. I contributed to the blowout with a 16-yard touchdown run.

Once I was taken out of the game, it was great to stand on the sidelines and watch the defense pitch a shutout.

The last game of the season against Miami was a really fun game. First of all, the game was played on December 1. The weather in Miami in December sure was nicer than it was in South Bend. I remember being on the beach with some of my teammates, messing around and having fun. Everyone on that beach looked like a model.

One of our biggest challenges of the season was our third game against Michigan State. The Spartans were always a hard team to play against. They tried to beat us to death. They would hit you hard enough to knock the doo-doo out of you.

We grinded out a 14-10 victory with touchdowns from Wayne Bullock and Pete Demmerle. The big difference on the day was our stellar defense.

The 1973 Irish defense was loaded with players like Sherm Smith along with reserves Willie Fry; Mike Parker; Tom Lopienski; Jay Achterhoff; Tony Novakov; Bob Zanot; and Mike Webb.

The biggest blowout of the season came in Game Five against Army. We steamrolled them 62-3. That was one of those games where Ara really made an effort not to embarrass our opponent. He took the starters out early, put in the second team and then removed them for the third team. The third team ran the ball just about every play and Army still could not stop us.

I finished the game gaining 49-yards on nine carries (5.4-yards-per-carry) and scored twice with touchdown runs of one-yard and six-yards.

In the seventh game of the season against Pittsburgh, I was matched up against Tony Dorsett, who would go on to win the Heisman Trophy and lead Pitt to the National Championship in 1976. I also got to play against my Gilmour backfield mate, Dave Janasek, "Mr. Inside," again.

I told the guys on our defense that they had to make sure to tackle Dorsett so that I could have more yards than him. Whenever I was matched up against a talented running back, I always took it as a personal challenge to gain more yards than he did.

Dorsett was still small and skinny as a freshman, but he was a great tailback. I have to admit that I was a little jealous of the fact that Dorsett was allowed to use jukes and dance around when he carried the ball, while Notre Dame running backs were only allowed to run north-to-south.

I had 10-carries for 55-yards (5.5-yards-per-carry). Dorsett did outgain me by quite a bit, finishing the game with 209-yards on 29 carries (7.2-yards-per-carry). He never scored a touchdown, though. And the most important thing was that Notre Dame won 31-10.

Throughout the game, I kept on taking handoffs on a draw play. We kept running the same play over and over because Pittsburgh could not stop it. I was gaining a lot of yards and talking a bunch of slop to the Pitt defense. Then, I took a handoff on another draw play, got hit and, boom! There went my front two teeth.

I got up and started yelling, "Where's my front teeth? Where's my front teeth?"

Well, I was talking slop, so that was really on me.

I spent a few days walking around the Notre Dame campus without my two front teeth. There were a lot of jokes about what I wanted for Christmas, referencing the, "All I want for Christmas is my two front teeth," Christmas carol.

I eventually got in to see a dentist. They drilled a hole in my mouth and put in caps. How is this for irony, though: I had to have all of my teeth pulled because of diabetes, except those two front teeth. The caps are still attached!

I had a good game in our 44-7 win against Navy running for 46-yards on seven carries (6.6-yards-per-carry) and scoring a 20-yard touchdown before being removed because of the route.

I put up a multiple touchdown game against Airforce. On 11 carries I gained 67-yards (6.1-yards-per-carry) and scored a six-yard touchdown and a four-yard touchdown, helping the Irish win 48-15.

There were some things about the 1973 season that were frustrating for me. In 1973, we changed our offense to a Wing-T. Within that system, the Irish had four outstanding running backs with Wayne Bullock, Art Best, Al Samuel and me. I wound up being used as a decoy on a lot of plays which really ticked me off. That said, it did open up a lot of plays for Wayne, Art and Al, all of whom had great statistical seasons.

Wayne finished the regular season with 752-yards on 162 carries (4.6-yards-per-carry) and scored 10 touchdowns. Art gained 700-yards on 118 carries (5.9-yards-per-carry) and scored three touchdowns in the regular season. Al ended the regular season with 221-yards on 33 carries (6.7-yards-per-carry) and scored two touchdowns.

I still had a good statistical regular season with 586-yards on 102 carries (5.7-yards-per-carry) and scored seven touchdowns.

Other running backs who picked up yards for us included Tim Simon, Gary Diminick, John Gambone, and Greg Hill.

A big part of the success of our running backs in 1973 was our fantastic offensive line. Even our reserves were outstanding with players like John O'Donnell; Max Wasilevich; Tom Bolger; Tom Laney; Dennis Lozzi; Mike McBride; Vince Klees; and Dan Morrin.

What made 1973 such an individually successful season for me was that I scored two touchdowns at the biggest moments of the two most important games of the year.

The first of those moments came on October 27, 1973, in South Bend against USC.

CHAPTER 12

All my life, even when I was just playing football on the street, I wanted to be the best running back on the field. That continued through high school and into college. My ability to accomplish that was limited a bit my junior season when I was often being used as a decoy, but I always had the same mindset. If I was going to line up in the backfield and take handoffs, I wanted to be better than the guy taking handoffs on the other team. I always believed I was the fastest guy on the field and that the defense could not catch me. I just had to run and do what I did best.

I felt that way even more strongly when Notre Dame was playing against a tailback with a lot of hype. It had been very important to me to have more yards than Tony Dorsett in the game against Pitt. But there was no one in the world I wanted to beat more than Anthony Davis.

I had spent the entire offseason thinking about Davis sliding on his knees and hotdogging against us in 1972. I spent many nights dreaming about getting to play USC and Davis again. By the time the Notre Dame vs. USC game rolled around on October 27, 1973, I was ready to kill him.

There was electricity in the South Bend air in the week leading up to the game. Students created effigies of Davis and hung them up around campus. We had a pep rally before the game, and it was packed. I could not have been more pumped up.

The Notre Dame vs. USC rivalry may be the greatest and most historic in college football and maybe in all of sports. I certainly think it is.

According to legend, it began after the wives of Knute Rockne and USC athletic director Gywnn Wilson got to talking during a game between Notre Dame and Nebraska. Rockne, Notre Dame's most legendary coach, was skeptical of playing a home-and-home series with USC because of the travel involved. Back then, the teams took trains to games. Mrs. Wilson eventually convinced Mrs. Rockne that a trip to a warm place like California every two years would be a great way to get out of the South Bend winters. And thus, the rivalry was born.

The Irish and the Trojans met for the first time on December 4, 1926 in Los Angeles Memorial Coliseum. Notre Dame won 13-12. The game has been played every year since except 1943-1945 because of World War II, and 2020 when the Pac-12 Conference cancelled its nonconference schedule because of the Covid-19 pandemic.

Heading into the 1973 season, the Trojans had become a bugaboo for the Irish and Coach Parseghian.

In Ara's first year at Notre Dame in 1964, the Irish lost to the Trojans 20-17. Notre Dame did beat USC in 1965 (28-7) and in 1966 (51-0). That was the last time Ara and Notre Dame had won, though. USC beat Notre Dame 24-7 in 1967. The Irish and Trojans then tied each other in 1968 (21-21) and 1969 (14-14). After that, the Trojans went on a three-year winning streak: 1970 (38-28), 1971 (28-14), 1972 (45-23).

With six years passing since Notre Dame's last win against USC, including losing three consecutive games, the narrative became that Ara could not win the big game against the Trojans.

We took the field that day before an announced sellout crowd of 59,075. The sky was grey. *The New York Times* called it, "Grantland Rice weather." The reference was to the famous sportswriter who had eulogized Notre Dame for the New York Herald-Tribune in 1924. Following a game against Army, Grantland Rice had written: "Outlined against a blue, gray October sky, the Four Horseman rode again."

As we took the field that day, Notre Dame was the No. 8 ranked team in the country. USC was the defending National Champions from 1972, and the No. 6 ranked team in the nation.

The 1973 matchup was a battle befitting the historic rivalry.

The tone for the game was set right away. On USC's first offensive play, the Trojans threw a quick screen to Lynn Swann. Our freshman strong safety, Luther Bradley, read the play perfectly and tackled Swann for a loss, hitting him so hard that Swann's helmet came flying off.

At the end of the first quarter, USC had a 7-3 lead following a 32-yard field goal by kicker Bob Thomas, and a one-yard TD run by Anthony Davis. At halftime, we led 13-7 after another 32-yard field goal and a one-yard quarterback keeper by Tom Clements.

With 11:25 remaining in the third quarter, we still had a 13-7 lead with the ball on our own 15-yard-line.

On Notre Dame's first offensive play of the second half, the Irish called a high-low-sweep. The high-low-sweep was one of our most dynamic plays. We ran it from a double tight end set. It went to both the left and the right side with either one of the split backs getting the ball. In that moment, my number was called to go around the left end.

Before the snap I went into motion, moving from my position on the right side toward the left.

Mark Brenneman snapped the ball and fired off the line, taking out the USC noseguard.

Tom Clements took the snap, faked as if we were going to do a fullback dive, turned, and put the ball into my chest. I grabbed the ball and already had a full head of steam moving toward the outside of the line.

Our offensive tackles, Steve Sylvester and Steve Neece, completely sealed off their men.

Just before I reached the line of scrimmage, I picked up an out-of-this-world block from Art Best. From his slot position on the left side of the line, Art blew up the USC defensive end. Art hit the defensive end so hard that the lineman fell into USC's defensive tackle, knocking both men out of the play.

With that block, I was able to easily find the edge and turn up field.

Tight end Dave Casper had released from the line of scrimmage and leveled the USC middle linebacker, who would have been

45

coming across the field to meet me.

Offensive guards Jerry DiNardo and Frank Pamarico were pulling from the line of scrimmage. They got into the second level of the USC defense and each knocked down a USC defender.

I was not surprised that the blocks were there. We had called the right play at the right time, and it was exactly how it was supposed to be. Just like in my dreams.

With room to run, I was able to stand straight up and just go. At the 33-yard-line, USC defensive back Danny Reece caught up to me. I did just the smallest of stutter steps. It was enough to throw off Reece's timing. Reece got his hands on my shoulder pads, but I had a step on him, and I was able to break the arm tackle without it even slowing me down.

And then, I was gone.

Call it egotistical, but I knew in that moment that there was no one who could catch me.

The only thing I saw was open field and the goal line out before me. I was just running. I did not know that there were three USC defenders chasing me. One of them was Reece. After I had broken Reece's tackle, he continued to pursue me, and just barely missed tackling me again as he dove for my feet at the 9-yard-line.

Exactly 12 seconds passed from when the ball was snapped until I crossed the goal line for an 85-yard touchdown. The PAT put us up 20-7.

Here is how the play was called on the CBS Broadcast by Lindsey Nelson and Paul Hornung, a former Notre Dame running back who won the Heisman Trophy for the Irish in 1956 before going on to a Hall of Fame NFL career with the Green Bay Packers:

Lindsey Nelson: "11 minutes, 25 seconds remaining to be played in the third quarter. Notre Dame is leading 13-7. First-and-10 for the Irish at their own 15-yard-line. ... This is Penick. Penick! Penick! And Penick is at the 40, 35, 30."
Paul Hornung: "They're not going to get him!"
Lindsey Nelson: "Penick has gone all the way for a touchdown. ... 85-yards."

Paul Hornung: "And he is mobbed in the endzone."

The broadcast cut immediately to a slow-motion replay.

Paul Hornung: "Let's take a look. Eric Penick coming of age. The longest run he's had since (being) in a Notre Dame uniform, and he breaks it. Well, I think Ara Parseghian has been waiting for this young man to do this. And he couldn't have picked it at a more beautiful time. Penick goes 85 for the score. And watch this. Whooo."

Lindsey Nelson: "Notre Dame ran out of a double tight end set. They had Casper and (Robin) Webber in, in a double tight end set. As Eric Penick broke it for 85-yards and the touchdown. And this stadium is a bedlam."

As soon as I crossed the goal line, I jumped up in joy. Because it was a huge game against USC, Notre Dame had allowed some spectators to watch the game from the field. I was swarmed by fans, patting me on the back and screaming. Then, my teammates were out on the field, and I was surrounded by them. The moment was pure chaos and pure joy.

The most important thing to me was that Ara ran onto the field and hugged me. He had never hugged me before, but he hugged me then. I will never forget that. It was so special. Ara wanted to beat USC so much. And I wanted to beat USC for my coach.

Afterward, on the sideline, someone asked me, "Why didn't you slide on your knees?"

"Because this is Notre Dame," I said. "This is how we do things."

After the touchdown, with the way our defense was playing, the game was effectively iced.

USC made the score 20-14 with a 27-yard touchdown pass from Pat Haden to Lynn Swann. We then went up by two scores with yet another 32-yard field goal.

The final score: Notre Dame 23, USC 14.

I finished the game with 118-yards rushing. Davis rushed for just 55-yards. Not only had I outgained Davis, I had rushed for 50-

yards more than the entire USC team.

I do not really remember much about the night after that game. I do not think I went out that night. My guess is that I just stayed in my room and soaked up the moment. I do remember lying in my bed that night, exhausted from the game.

I felt happy that we had beaten USC. And I felt extremely happy that we had beaten Anthony Davis.

A week later, the cover of "Sports Illustrated" featured the Notre Dame defense tackling Anthony Davis. I was quoted in the article. Here are the final paragraphs of the story:

Afterward everyone wanted to know what kind of a move Penick had put on Danny Reece at the 35.

"On who?" he said. "I didn't know anybody had me. I didn't feel a thing. In fact, I can't remember anything except being loose and running it out. It's all by instinct."

Someone suggested that perhaps Penick should have completed his 85-yard trip by sliding on his knees in the USC endzone.

The 213-pound junior recoiled at the thought. "On my knees?" he said in disgust. "I'm no hot dog. This is Notre Dame."

CHAPTER 13

The world of college football was totally different in 1973. In today's world—as of 2023—there is a true National Championship Game. Back in 1973, it was all subjective. Voters would decide whether this team would be a National Champion, or that team would be a National Champion, most often without the teams ever even playing against each other.

Fate and the stars aligned to make the 1973 Sugar Bowl a de facto National Championship game.

The Irish came into the Bowl game ranked as the Nation's No. 3 team with a 10-0 record. Alabama came into the game ranked as the Nation's No. 1 team with a 10-0 record.

Oklahoma was ranked ahead of Notre Dame in the polls. They should not have been. In coach Barry Switzer's first season with Oklahoma, the Sooners, were 10-0-1 after tying USC 7-7. Even with a higher ranking than us, the Big East Conference had placed Oklahoma on probation before the season for "recruiting irregularities," and Oklahoma was banned from Bowl Games in 1973 and 1974.

In another testament to how different college football was back then, the UPI Coaches Poll named Alabama National Champions *before* the Sugar Bowl took place. The premature UPI Coaches Poll was not tabulated again even after the outcomes of the Bowl Games, making the polling a mockery.

All of that was just background noise.

Everyone in the world of college football knew that the 1973 Sugar Bowl between Notre Dame and Alabama would determine the National Championship.

There was no one single moment during the 1973 season

when I knew that we were going to be playing for the National Championship. It was all cumulative. We continued winning games and winning games. Following our 44-0 win over Miami, we were selected to face 'Bama in the Sugar Bowl.

We ended the season against Miami on December 1. The Sugar Bowl was scheduled for December 31, New Year's Eve.

The month before the game was a grind. A very, very hard grind. We all had to be ready to play. We practiced like we had never practiced before. We practiced in the snow. When the coaches allowed us to practice inside, we had to keep our sweats on for additional heat-training. That December was so tough. It was very fun, but those were tough times.

I do not even remember Christmas that year. My teammates say that the football team had to stay on campus, which makes sense. All I knew was that we had to practice. Practice. Practice. Practice. And get ready for the Bowl Game. That is all that existed in the world for me.

The Notre Dame football team flew down to New Orleans several days before the game. Walking off the plane, I knew, inevitably, that we were going to be National Champs.

I did not mess around in New Orleans. I had made that mistake before the Orange Bowl the previous year, and it cost me the first half of that game. I had grown up by December of 1973. I was older and more mature. I knew what was important. I knew we had a chance to make history. I was not going to go out and act silly and have fun. I wanted to play football. I wanted to win. Adventures in Sin City could wait until after the Sugar Bowl.

One night, before the game was to be played, the Notre Dame and Alabama football players had a joint dinner together.

The banquet was attended by George Wallace. The Alabama Governor was famous for his 1963 Inaugural Address in which he said, "In the name of the greatest people that have ever trod this earth, I draw the line in the dust and toss the gauntlet before the feet of tyranny, and I say segregation now, segregation tomorrow, segregation forever."

As a college student, I still did not know everything that I would later learn about the Civil Rights movement and its history. Everyone knew about Governor Wallace, though.

This was after Wallace's presidential run in 1972. During that campaign, on May 15, 1972, Wallace had been shot four times by Arthur Bremer in Laurel, Maryland. Wallace had survived the assassination attempt, but was confined to a wheelchair for the rest of his life.

While running for President, Wallace had announced that he no longer supported segregation and that he had always been a "moderate" on racial matters.

"Oh, wow," I kept thinking to myself, as I broke bread in the same room as a famous racist, "Are you serious? Wow."

And do you know what I did when the Alabama Governor was shaking the hands of all the players from his wheelchair?

I shook the hand of the Alabama Governor and famous racist George Wallace. I looked him in the eye and said, "Thank you for having us here."

What else could I do? What else could I say? Was I going to go and spit on him, or hit him, or something? No. My mother raised me to always be the bigger man and be the bigger person. So, I was the bigger man and the bigger person.

That was not the only moment when racial tension crept onto the canvass of the Sugar Bowl.

In the days before the game, I was contacted by the National Association for the Advancement of Colored People (NAACP). They asked me to boycott the game.

I did not even consider it. It was absolutely not even a consideration.

"Are you kidding me?" I asked. "I'm going to prove that we (Black men) belong on the field. I can't do that by not playing in the game. I am getting a great education from Notre Dame. I'm not boycotting the game. I am a Notre Dame Man!"

I turned the request down strongly enough that the NAACP left me alone after that.

Finally, after all the practicing and all the racial drama, New Year's Eve arrived.

It was Gameday.

CHAPTER 14

Played on New Year's Eve before an announced sellout crowd of 85,161, the 1973 Sugar Bowl was a game for the ages. Notre Dame and Alabama spent 60 minutes trading knockout punches. We were going back and forth, back and forth, back and forth.

The matchup saw two fabled, Hall of Fame coaches face off against each other with Coach Parseghian and Alabama Coach Paul "Bear" Bryant. It was akin to Ulysses S. Grant and Robert E. Lee commanding their armies against one another. That Sugar Bowl may have been the most strategically coached game ever. Every moment of the game was a chess move between two grandmasters.

With 3:19 remaining in the first quarter, Notre Dame went up 6-0 on a 6-yard touchdown run by Wayne Bullock. The Irish missed the PAT, though.

Alabama answered with a 6-yard TD run by Randy Billingsley with 7:30 remaining in the second quarter. Following the PAT, the Tide led 7-6.

Al Hunter then took the ensuing kickoff to the house with an electrifying 93-yard touchdown return. Coach Parseghian decided to go for the two-point conversion and Tom Clements found Pete Demerle with a pass in the endzone, putting us up 14-7.

With 39 seconds remaining before halftime, the Tide brought the score to 14-10 on a 39-yard Bill Davis field goal.

As the second half got underway, Wilbur Jackson ran in a 5-yard touchdown for Alabama. The PAT gave the Crimson Tide a 17-14 lead with 11:02 remaining in the third quarter.

The Sugar Bowl really was just a fantastic game. It seemed to go by so fast and a lot of it just blurs in my mind.

I do not even remember when I fractured my ankle.

All I know is that sometime in the third quarter, I was brought down by a tackle and my left ankle got twisted beneath me. I have no idea how it happened, or when. At the time, my ankle hurt, but I did not mention the injury to anyone, or even get it taped. I thought that I just needed to let it loosen up. I certainly did not think that I had fractured it.

Some moments from the Sugar Bowl, I will remember until the day that I die.

With just under three minutes remaining in the third quarter, the Crimson Tide had the ball on their own 19-yard-line, still holding onto their 17-14 lead.

I was standing on the sidelines trying to loosen up my ankle as I watched Alabama snap the ball.

Our defensive line had been getting a great push throughout the game from George Hayduk and Gary Potempa and defensive ends Jim Stock and Ross Browner.

On this play, defensive lineman Kevin Nosbusch beat his man off the ball so badly that he was through the line of scrimmage before the play had even begun to develop.

Tim Rudnick, Reggie Barnett and Mike Townsend reacted to the play and began creeping up from their defensive back positions.

Alabama handed the ball off to Mike Stock. Nosbusch had a clean shot at the Alabama running back and just blew him up. The hit sprung the ball free.

Linebacker Drew Mahalic was flying toward the play from the right side of the field on a blitz. Mahalic snagged the ball out of the air at the 20-yard-line without breaking stride. He immediately hurdled the wreckage of Stock and Nosbusch, cut toward the left sideline and picked up eight-yards before being brought down at the Alabama 12-yard-line.

My ankle was still bothering me, but I was going back out onto the field. There was no way I was going to watch from the sidelines. We had to score a touchdown.

In a defining moment of the most important game of my life, Notre Dame called a high-low-sweep. I was getting the ball. It was the same play the Irish had called two months earlier against USC when I went 85-yards for the touchdown.

Lined up on the right side in a three-point stance, I could not feel my fractured ankle. I was so hyped up, and my adrenalin was so high that I did not feel anything.

Art Best went into motion. The ball was snapped. I sprinted toward the left side of the field. Clements faked the fullback dive, spun and handed me the ball. As I reached the line of scrimmage, there was no one there. The offensive line had opened up a gigantic hole. I flashed through the line and was able to stand up and accelerate right away, carrying the ball in my left arm.

Dave Casper sprinted from his tight end position and was out in front of me. At the 5-yard-line, Casper first blocked an Alabama defensive back to the ground. Then, as Casper was losing his balance, he was able to get his pads on a second Alabama defensive back, knocking him out of the play as well.

Without hyperbole, that block by "Ghost" was the greatest block in the history of college football. I say that because someone may someday throw a block that good again, but no one will ever have a better block. It is simply not possible.

I read Casper's blocks, bounced the run to the sideline, and I was gone, 12-yards into the endzone, untouched.

As I crossed the goal line, I raised my right hand in absolute triumph. I was going so fast that I had to run into the padded wall behind the endzone to slow my momentum. I was first greeted by a group of Notre Dame cheerleaders who had poured into the endzone. Then my teammates swarmed me. We were all jumping up and down, elated to have taken the lead.

As I ran toward the sidelines, I high fived several spectators who were down on the field. The television camera zoomed in on me. I had an obvious limp from my fractured left ankle. I did not even feel it, though.

Here is how the play was called on ABC by Chris Schenkel, Howard Cosell and Bud Wilkinson.

Chris Schenkel: "Now to test the Alabama defense at the 12 of the Crimson Tide. First down Notre Dame. Best in motion. Penick, back in the lineup. Penick … scores! Notre Dame has the lead."

Howard Cosell: "Shades of the 85-yard touchdown run play against the University of Southern California. … Counter play against the flow, beautifully executed."

Chris Schenkel: "And as we were talking at the start of the show, Howard, it's that fullback fake up the middle that freezes those linebackers. And when you get the hole open and turn the corner, it was exactly the same play that broke the back of the Trojans."

Bud Wilkinson: "As expected a fantastic game. Five lead changes thus far. We're still in the third quarter with two and a half minutes to go."

After the extra point, the Fighting Irish led 21-17.

Alabama would retake the lead on a 25-yard TD catch by quarterback Richard Todd on a halfback pass from Mike Stock. The Tide missed the PAT, though, and led just 23-21 with 9:33 remaining in the fourth quarter.

Their missed PAT wound up being huge.

With 5:13 remaining in the game, Notre Dame lined up for a 19-yard field goal. Joe Alvarado delivered a perfect snap, Brian Doherty had a steady hold, and the kick by Bob Thomas was good, putting us up 24-23.

Another moment from the Sugar Bowl that I will always remember came with 2:12 remaining in the fourth quarter. Notre Dame was still holding onto our 24-23 lead. Alabama had pinned us on our own 3-yard-line, and we were facing a third down and eight-yards-to-go.

Notre Dame called for a play action pass. The play was designed for Clements to fake the handoff to me and throw downfield to tight end Robin Weber. If we completed the pass, we could run out the clock and the National Championship was ours. If we did not complete the pass, we would have to punt. That would probably set Alabama up with good field position, and the Crimson Tide would have a chance to win the game with just a field goal.

Robin was my good buddy. In the huddle he looked at me and

said, "Fake it like you've never faked it before, Eric."

I lined up knowing that I had to do the best acting job of my life to help us secure the National Championship.

When the ball was snapped, Clements turned and faked the handoff to me. I plunged through the middle of the line of scrimmage. I was convincing enough that not only did the Alabama defenders believe I had the ball, but the television camera focused on me. It was not until I spun out of the line that the television camera realized that I did not have the ball.

I watched as Robin made an over the shoulder catch at the 30-yard-line. When Robin was finally tackled out of bounds at our 38-yard-line, I knew we had won the game.

We ran out the clock and the National Championship was ours.

I finished the Sugar Bowl with 9 carries for 28-yards and a touchdown.

Fans stormed the field as I celebrated with my teammates. We were all jumping up and down and patting each other on the back and doing all kinds of silly stuff right next to Ara. It was the most exciting moment of my life.

My Notre Dame Fighting Irish team winning the National Championship was a dream come true.

Now, there is one addendum to Notre Dame's 1973 National Championship season.

The absurd UPI Coaches Poll voted Alabama as the No. 1 team in the nation after the regular season and did not cast its votes again. The embarrassment of proclaiming Alabama National Champions caused the UPI Coaches Poll to change its voting structure the next season so that the final vote was held after Bowl Games.

Still, the Crimson Tide can technically make a claim to be National Champions in 1973. I promise you, though, there is not an Alabama player who would ever make that claim while standing in the same room with a Notre Dame Man.

CHAPTER 15

I thought that the 1974 season was going to be a great year. The Irish were the defending National Champs and I had had a standout junior season. I do not know if I could have been in the conversation for the Heisman Trophy, but I was sure I could be an All American. In fact, I went into the 1974 season as a preseason All American.

The voters had no idea what had happened several months earlier during a spring practice.

The stress fracture in my ankle that I suffered during the National Championship game never fully healed. I look back now and wish I had paid attention to it. I did not tell anybody, though. Back in the day, you did not tell anyone when you got hurt. You just kept playing. And when spring came around, the ankle did not feel too bad. I thought I was OK.

I was not.

During a normal spring practice on a normal day in South Bend, I took a handoff. I was running the high-low-sweep. It was the play on which I had gone 85-yards into the endzone against USC. It was the play on which I had scored the 12-yard touchdown against Alabama. It was *my* play.

As I ran through the line, I distinctly remember one of the coaches shouting, "Somebody get him! Somebody get him! You're going to let him run all over you? Somebody get him!"

Then, someone hit me high and someone else hit me low. My body torqued from being hit at different angles. As I fell to the ground, my left foot stayed in place. With the joint already weakened by the stress fracture, it did not stand a chance. I felt my ankle break completely.

Lying on the ground, I grabbed my ankle and shouted, "My money! My money!"

Everybody laughed that I was shouting about my money rather than my leg. Actually, it is pretty funny. But that was the first thing that came into my mind. I grew up a poor kid from Cleveland. Football was supposed to be the path out of that for my family and me. As I felt my ankle break that day, I knew exactly what I stood to lose.

In modern football, coaches are much better at protecting players. Especially star position players. In the new millennium, I would have never taken a serious hit like that in a spring practice. It is what it is, though. Back in those days, we had full contact scrimmages. That is just how it was.

Hell, if I had paid attention to the pain of the stress fracture, if I had told somebody what had happened, I probably would not have broken my ankle anyway.

We did have full contact practices back then, though. And I did not tell anybody that I still had pain in my ankle. I got hurt. And I wish I had not gotten hurt. Period.

I had to have surgery. The orthopedic process of fixing an ankle in the 1970s was a lot more primitive and a lot worse than it is today. The only thing the doctors could think to do was cut my ankle open and put a bunch of screws in it.

I had never been hurt before. Never. It changed my whole life. I was a different person after I got hurt. My brain was screwed, basically.

I went out and partied and drank and acted out and did all kinds of stupid stuff.

I was able to work myself back into shape by the next fall, but the ankle never healed right. Eventually, complications from the break and the archaic surgery would lead to vascular problems which, combined with diabetes, caused me to lose my leg.

After that spring practice, I was never the same player, and I was never the same person. My life went downhill from that moment, and it did not stop going downhill for a long time.

CHAPTER 16

As a senior in 1974, I was not as good as I had been the year before. Not even close. My ankle was never right again after I broke it. I did not have the burst of speed I had always had. I was just a little bit slower. For a player who ran the ball like I did, that little bit of lost speed was the difference between being a star and barely being good enough to get into an occasional game.

I was able to make traveling squad as a senior. But I was no longer a starter. I played in just four regular season games. I had 12 carries for all of 14-yards. I caught one pass for two-yards. I did not score a touchdown.

We had a talented running back corps in 1974. Along with our starters Al Samuel and Wayne Bullock, Ara's son, Mike Parseghian, Tom Parise, Russ Kornman, Terry Eurick, Ron Goodman, Mark McLane, Jim Weiler, John Rufo, and Richard Allocco were tailbacks who could all run without the pain I was battling.

Al Wujciak was a new starter on our veteran offensive line.

We added new receivers like Ken MacAfee and Kevin Doherty.

New contributors to our veteran defense included: Randy Harrison; John Dubenetzky; Marv Russell; Tom Eastman; Randy Payne; Jeff Weston; Doug Becker; Mike Banks; Nick Fedorenko; Joe Pszeracki; Pete Johnson; Ted Burgmeier; Ernie Hughes; and John Galanis. Linebacker Gene Smith, from my hometown of Cleveland, would go on to become the Athletic Director at Ohio State University.

Notre Dame was still good in 1974, but we were not elite in the same way we had been in 1973. The Irish went 10-2 and finished the year ranked as the No. 4 team in the Nation by the Associated Press.

In September, we dropped a home game to Purdue 31-20.

I got into the final game of the regular season against USC in Los Angeles, but was unable to do much.

It was a brutal day for the Irish. We took a 24-0 lead, then USC blew us off the field, scoring 55 unanswered points to win 55-24. It was heartbreaking to watch Notre Dame lose that game and think about what I had done against the Trojans the year before.

I also got into my final collegiate game in the Orange Bowl on January 1, 1975 against Alabama. The Tide came into the game undefeated, knowing that a win would give them the National Championship.

The Irish once again wrecked Bama's hopes of a title with a 13-11 victory.

I even got one last bright moment as a college football running back. On Notre Dame's second possession in the first quarter, I took a handoff around the end for eight-yards and a first down.

The Irish sealed the Orange Bowl victory with Frank Allocco becoming the last quarterback to ever take a snap for Coach Parseghian after Clements went down with an injury.

Ara retired after the game and Dan Devine took over as head coach.

Coach Devine and the other Notre Dame coaches wanted me to come back to play one more season in 1975 as a fifth-year senior.

By then, I was ready to move on. I just did not want to go to school anymore.

Had I stayed, I would have been part of a very talented 1975 team.

Rick Slager would go on to win the QB position, beating out future legend Joe Montana.

Pat McLaughlin became Notre Dame's kicker.

I would miss the moment immortalized in the film "Rudy" when defensive back Pat Sarb voluntarily gave up his position so that Daniel "Rudy" Ruettiger could dress for the last game of the season, and defensive end Tony Zappala ran off the field on his own initiative and told "Rudy" to replace him for the final play of the game.

Because I had gone to summer school, I had more than enough credits to graduate on time. I completed the promise that I had made to my mother and grandmother and earned my degree from the University of Notre Dame.

Is it possible that my life could have been different had I gone to a different college? Maybe.

I enjoyed my time at Notre Dame, though. I had my ups and downs there. I had my issues. Everyone does. But I did enjoy my time at Notre Dame.

I loved being on the Notre Dame football team. We had a bunch of great guys. The defense stopped everyone from scoring against us. The offense put the ball in the end zone. The lineman opened up big holes for me to run through and gain yards. It was 11 guys on the field at a time, and everyone did their jobs.

I liked my coaches, and I think they liked me. I still talk to some of the coaches. Assistant Coach Mike Stock called me just the other day on my birthday. I loved Coach Parseghian, of course.

I finished my Notre Dame career with 1,327-yards on 238 carries (5.6-yards-per-carry) and 12 touchdowns in the regular season. I also gained 84-yards on 18 carries (4.6-yards-per-carry) and scored an additional touchdown in the bowl games. And that was in a time before the modern day spread offense had college football running backs putting up gaudy numbers.

My Irish teams won a bunch of games from 1972-74, compiling a combined record of 29-5. And, of course, Notre Dame won the 1973 National Championship.

My entire life, people have always wanted to talk to me about the National Championship. I love that. The people who went to Notre Dame, those people still remember me. That means so much to me. I have friends from Notre Dame who still call me every day. My time at Notre Dame did not end the way I wanted it to end. But I had incredible moments there. I left South Bend with a Notre Dame degree.

The bottom line is, I am a Notre Dame Man.

CHAPTER 17

Under today's college football rules, players are allowed to leave for the NFL after their third collegiate season. In the early 1970s, players had to complete four years before entering the NFL draft.

Had I been able to leave college after my junior season, I very well could have been a first-round draft pick. I had the physique, the 40-yard-dash speed, and I looked great on film with my 85-yard touchdown run against USC, among other impressive plays.

It says a lot about how much potential I had that even though I did not play almost at all as a senior, I was still on the radar of many NFL teams.

I was invited to a version of today's NFL combine in Alabama. I remember running a 4.54 40-yard-dash, which is lightning fast, even by today's standards. I did workouts for a few teams, including my hometown Cleveland Browns. I was never as fast or as quick as I wanted to be. My ankle was not right and because of that, everything was just a little bit off with me physically. I take 99-percent of the blame for that. I did not practice right or work hard enough to get myself and my ankle in shape to play.

The Denver Broncos took a shot on me, selecting me in the 13th round with the 329th overall pick in the 1975 NFL draft. I really did not care which team drafted me. Being from Cleveland, I would have liked to go to the Browns, but they did not draft me. With the Broncos selecting me, I knew that I would at least get to try to play in the NFL.

My dream had always been to play professional football and make money for myself and my family doing it. Without being healthy, I was not sure I would be able to make the Broncos squad. There was nothing to do but give it a shot.

Broncos training camp was tough. The heat did not bother me, but with Denver's 5,279-feet of elevation, I had trouble catching my breath (as did just about everyone else).

The Broncos trainers gave me ankle stretches to do and taped my ankle up like a horse before every game. I could not cut off of it the way I wanted to, though.

Still, I felt like I played OK during the preseason. The coaches wanted me to be on the kickoff team, which I really hated. Other than that, carrying the ball as an NFL running back was really fun.

I was Denver's leading rusher in a preseason game against the Chicago Bears. To this day, I still remember taking a handoff on a sweep and seeing that I had wide open field for days and days. I could not turn the corner, though. With my ankle, I just could not turn that corner.

I made it all the way through training camp.

Two bits of irony ended my life in football.

The first irony was that the Broncos acquired Tim Rudnick from the Baltimore Colts. Tim had been a Notre Dame defensive back and was a good buddy of mine. When the Broncos brought in my former teammate, they needed to clear a roster spot, so they waved me. I was replaced on the roster by Tim Rudnick. Of all people in the world, it was Tim Rudnick. I will never forget that.

The second irony was something I found out later. After seeing the way I ran against the Bears, Chicago's head coach, Abe Gibron, was interested in me. This was long before cellphones. The Bears did not know how to get ahold of me in Denver, so they filled the roster spot with someone else to compliment their new rookie running back, Walter Payton.

If there had been cellphones like there are now, the Bears would have been in contact with me right away. It just did not work out, though. I think about that every day. Well, not every day. But it sure felt awful finding out that I could have had another chance to make an NFL roster.

Once I was released from the Broncos, I received interest from the Hamilton Tiger Cats of the Canadian Football League. I went up to Canada for a visit as I was considering the opportunity. My mother was unenthusiastic about it.

"Get a job," my mom said. "Go start your career. You're nearing 30-years-old."

I was still only 22-years-old, of course, but I listened to my mother's advice.

I decided that the best thing for me as a person was to give up football and challenge myself as a businessman.

With the success I had in my business career, I never regretted listening to my mother and giving up the game of football.

CHAPTER 18

Football was gone and over, and I had to take care of my family. That was the way I looked at my life after I was released by the Broncos.

I was definitely ready to move on from football. I had had my opportunity to play, and I had fun doing it, but I was excited for my next opportunity: Using my Notre Dame degree.

While I was trying to make the Broncos squad, A.C. was living down in Birmingham, Alabama with her family. She stayed there while I tried to start my business career in Denver. There were several people in Denver who I had known at Notre Dame, and the Mile High City seemed full of possibilities and adventure as I set out to begin my new life.

One of my acquaintances was a girl I had known from Notre Dame named Condoleezza Rice.

At the time, I could not have imagined that under the presidency of George W. Bush, Condoleezza would become the United States Secretary of State from 2005-2009. For several years, she was the most powerful woman in the country. She and I never talked about politics, and I had no idea that she was even politically conservative. I hung out with her because it was fun to have someone I had known at Notre Dame, a fellow Black student from Notre Dame no less, in my new city.

Years later, in her autobiography, "Extraordinary, Ordinary People: A Memoir of Family" Condoleezza wrote:

Eric had a reputation as a "bad boy."

"What the hell?" I said, aloud when I read that. "You're going to put that in writing?"

So, in my book, I will tell you that Condoleezza was kind of a square!

As I started my career in Denver, my resume consisted of my Notre Dame degree and some manual labor that I had done while I was going to school.

My first job in college was working construction and knocking down cafeteria walls while back home in Cleveland. The job had been so awful that I never went home during the summer again.

I got a much better job the next summer. My friend Dwight Clay, who played on the Irish basketball team and was one of the first people I ever met at Notre Dame in Cavanaugh Hall, invited me to spend a few weeks in Pittsburgh with him. I stayed in Dwight's house with his family, and we worked as laborers for a beer company.

I really cannot remember which beer company it was. I think it was either Pabst or Schlitz (not that it matters, since all of those beers are really just piss-water anyway). Dwight and I were loading beer into trucks all day. The job was great for getting in shape, and it had the added benefit of free beer. Whenever the laborers had a break, or took lunch, we got to drink some beer.

With a degree from Notre Dame, I no longer needed to make my living doing manual labor.

One of my first jobs in Denver was at a Ford Dealership. Mike Naughton, a DB on our National Championship Notre Dame team, helped me get hired as a business analyst there. I eventually took the same position at a Lincoln Mercury dealership.

A.C. and I stayed married through college and after I started working in Denver. Our daughter Erica was born in Alabama in 1977.

Around that time, I had gotten pretty mean, and A.C. and I were not getting along so well. I know in my heart that ruining my ankle played a big role in my marriage falling apart. I was happy before that. After I got hurt, I just went downhill with a bad attitude about a lot of stuff.

To be honest, I just did not like myself for a while.

I tried to get back together with A.C., but she was afraid of me because I was so mean, and she would not get back together with me. I remember going down to Alabama to try to talk with A.C. She would not come out of the house to see me. I had bought Erica a little Easy Bake Oven, and I gave it to her. As far as A.C. was concerned, though, our marriage was over. She was not going to come out of the house until I left.

After A.C. and I divorced, Erica was always available to me. Even when I moved down to Texas, she would come visit me. We would go to the track and run around with each other. She was on her high school track team, and she was fast, too. I still talk to Erica regularly on the phone and on Facebook. She is now a grandmother, which makes me a great grandfather.

CHAPTER 19

After A.C. and I split up, I started dating a girl named Michelle James. It is sort of funny, because Michelle went to Notre Dame, but I did not really talk to her when we were in school together. Michelle was living in Denver, though, and I got to know her while we were both there.

Michelle's father did not like me at all. He finally said to me, "You need to marry that girl. She ain't the kind of girl you just mess around with."

I did not like Michelle's father either, but I understood what he was saying.

I did wind up marrying Michelle. We moved to Aurora, Colorado, a town just outside of Denver. We had two kids together. Our son, Eric Paul, was born first, followed by our daughter, Mikel-Claire.

Michelle's father may not have liked me, but he did help me get a good job at the United Bank of Denver.

I had a really successful run at the United Bank of Denver over the next few years.

I started off doing credit analysis, which meant I was working with all the people who wanted loans. I had to go in front of what the bank called the Loan Committee to talk to them about the people with whom I was working. That was scary. Every time I went before the Loan Committee, I knew that I had to be prepared and have my ducks in order. If I did not have good answers to the questions the Loan Committee asked, they would tell me to come back. That meant the loan officer, my boss, would be really pissed with me because he would have to join me for the next meeting with the Loan Committee.

Eventually, I was promoted and became a loan officer myself, managing people who were doing the job I had been doing before.

I then became an account rep. I had fun doing that and had images of myself becoming a bigshot banker. My economics degree from Notre Dame gave me a good skillset and background. I was quickly promoted from account rep to correspondent banker.

As a correspondent banker, I dealt with other banks and set up lines of credit. At the time, my old buddy Dwight Clay was working in a similar field. Dwight and I wound up doing a lot of business together. That was really special for me. Dwight had grown up poor, just like I had. We had been athletes at Notre Dame, and we had both come up in the world, and we were making something of ourselves.

I call my time at United Bank of Denver enlightening. It was a great experience. Over the years, I learned more and more and more about the financial world.

My work in banking gave me the credentials to be hired at Prescott, Ball and Turben, a stockbrokerage firm. I began training to be a stockbroker, even going out onto the New York Stock Exchange floor to see how it worked.

I was still trying to be a stockbroker when I moved back home to Cleveland. Then, a close friend of mine who worked as a stockbroker died of a heart attack. He was a bit older than me, but not too much older than me.

Nowadays, I am old and I do not worry too much about dying. Back then, my friend dying of a heart attack scared the hell out of me. I did not want to die young, and the incident made me decide being a stockbroker was not for me.

Around this time, my marriage with Michelle began failing. I was still being mean. I was still not the man I wanted to be.

Eventually, Michelle and I divorced.

It was hard to connect with Eric Paul and Mikel-Claire after Michelle and I split up. Michelle was angry at me and angry about how our marriage had ended, and I did not get to spend much time with the kids.

I knew what was going on with the kids. I was proud to know that Eric Paul turned into a good football player. I never, ever disconnected with my kids. Never, ever. But it took me about 20 years to finally catch up with those kids on Facebook and start a relationship. I have their phone numbers now, and I talk with them.

Eric Paul and Mikel-Claire are still my kids. When they were babies, I used to carry them around and hold them on my chest. That cannot be forgotten by me. Ever.

CHAPTER 20

Back in Cleveland, I connected with a man named Ernie Green.

Ernie had played fullback and halfback for the Cleveland Browns for seven years (1962-1968), finishing his career with 3,204-yards rushing and 15 touchdown runs, and 2,036-yards receiving with 20 TD catches. He also made the pro bowl in 1966 and 1967.

I used to call him, "Uncle Ernie," because he always found a way to look out for me.

Uncle Ernie was on the board of Church's Fried Chicken, and he thought it would be a good fit for me.

"Man, you ain't going to make any kind of money kicking around finance," Uncle Ernie said. "Let me get you a job at Church's. With how smart you are, you'll move up really quick."

Uncle Ernie got me into a training program to become a manager at Church's. Once I went through the program, I started off as a store manager. I learned to do all the basic things that you have to do in the fast-food business.

A guy named Arnold Whitmore was a mentor to me at Church's. He taught me how to work hard and be my best at work every day. In some ways, Arnold reminded me of Coach Parseghian. Arnold made me look inward at myself as he pushed me as hard as I could be pushed.

I still remember Arnold showing me how to clean the windows with vinegar and a paper towel.

"You want the windows to sparkle, Eric," Arnold said.

"What the hell are you talking about, sparkle?" I asked.

"Yup. You want the windows to shine," Arnold insisted.

I had to have those windows cleaned all the time. Arnold would sit outside my store and watch me work and make sure I was doing what I needed to do.

At the time, the Church's uniform consisted of these stupid yellow/orange bowties with brown pants and dumb paper hats. Arnold taught me well, but I absolutely refused to ever wear that paper hat.

I was working at Church's one day when a man came into the restaurant, pointed a gun at me and demanded money.

It was the scariest moment of my life. The only time I have ever felt myself shaking from fear.

The robbery happened in the morning, before we opened the restaurant. I was in my office, counting out the money for the cash registers and getting ready for the day.

People were going in and out of the restaurant all morning. At one point, someone let a man into the restaurant so that he could use the bathroom.

When that man came out of the bathroom, he pulled a pistol.

The robber put all of my employees into the walk-in freezer.

My office door was closed, and I did not hear any of what was happening out in the restaurant.

What I had thought was going to be a peaceful morning was shattered as my office door burst open. The robber crossed the room before I understood what was happening. He put his pistol up against my head. I felt the barrel of the gun against my skin.

"Open the safe," the robber shouted.

I have been scared many times in my life, and by a lot of things, but I ain't never been scared like I was with a gun to my head.

Arnold had always told me that if I ever found myself in a robbery to never fight with a criminal over money.

"Money can be replaced," Arnold said. "Your life can't be."

I had no desire to fight with this robber about money. But I was so scared that I could not remember the combination to the safe.

"I can't remember the numbers," I said.

"Open the safe!" the robber shouted again, pressing the gun harder into my head.

"OK. Ok," I said. "Calm down. Calm down, and I'll get it open."

Well, I did finally get the safe open. As my hands found the numbers, my mind quieted down. I knew how much danger I was still in.

"Here's the money," I said, handing everything in the safe over to the robber. I pointed at the door to my office. "And now you've got to go. Take the back door out of the restaurant, and get out of here. You've got to go."

I must have been convincing enough. The robber took the money and got out of my office. I waited a few moments, until I was sure he had left the building. Then I walked out of my office and got my people out of the freezer.

The robber was gone, and he never did get caught.

Now, how is this for irony: The Church's restaurant where I had a gun pressed against my head, was right across the street from a police station.

The robbery was a really awful moment, but on the whole, I had a great experience working for Church's Fried Chicken. I was there for several years, managing stores, including what I believe was the first mall store that Church's had ever operated.

CHAPTER 21

While I was working at Church's Fried Chicken, I met the woman with whom I would finally get marriage right.

Her name was Sandra Poole. She worked with me at one of the Church's locations where I was stationed. She was a Master Merchant which was the highest rank you could be as a Church's Fried Chicken employee.

Sandra was so much smarter than I was as far as figuring out how to process things. We used to have to do inventory at Church's. You had to count the pieces of chicken and it would drive me nuts. Sandra was very aloof and for a while, she would not talk to me. I used to call her, "Cool Poole."

One day, though, Sandra helped me count the inventory. We started talking that day. Then, we started dating.

Eventually, I proposed. We went to a Justice of the Peace in Chicago and got married. Sandra was my heart. She and I would stay married for 37 years, until she passed away.

I had changed a lot by the time I met Sandra. I was not mean anymore. I was still cranky, for sure. And I was still disappointed in my life and how it had turned out. I had not been able to make it in track, or football, and I was not a lawyer like I had once wanted to be. But I was accomplishing a lot as a businessman. So, things were getting better, my mentality was better, and I was better.

The biggest reason Sandra and my marriage worked so well was that Sandra did not put up with my bullshit. Period.

Sandra and I started having kids soon after we got married, and we did not stop until we had had five children together. Our daughter, Jewel, was born first. Then came Eric Penick Jr. who we called Tony. After that, we had three more daughters: Krystal,

Amber and Jade.

So, if you are keeping track, that is eight total kids for me. I have so many damn kids, it's crazy. I used to tell everyone that I was just a good Catholic boy.

The hardest thing to learn is how to be a parent. There are no truly good books on it. And it changes each and every year. No matter what you do, it changes. Now, I am old, and I am listening to what my daughter Jewel tells me to do. From the beginning of their life until the end of your life, it is always different cycles.

I loved being a father. It was so much fun. You do not get eight hours of sleep in a night until the kids are no longer teenagers and are out of your house. You always worry about where they are, and what they are doing. But you love them no matter what. I cannot fully explain it. You love a kid so much that they become the essence of what you are. You see yourself in them.

I am telling you, having a child is the greatest thing you will ever do. And raising them with their mother is even better.

Now, I am a grandfather to a whole bunch of kids. Being a grandfather is different, but amazing in its own way. It is so much fun to see the lineage continue on.

When I was having children with Sandra, I decided that no matter what happened in my marriage, good or bad, up or down, I would never, ever leave their mother. I knew that I had to be committed to my wife. It was not just love, it was commitment. I had to make sure I was committed to that person. Of course I loved Sandra. But in some ways, my marriage to her was like my faith in God. You are either committed to God, and you love Him, or you are not committed to Him and you do not love Him. Commitment and love are for life.

While Sandra and I were having kids, I continued building up my resume, skillset and reputation at Church's. Then, I got recruited by Kentucky Fried Chicken. KFC offered me more money and a better job title, and I took it.

After they first hired me on, KFC had me based in Memphis, Tennessee to work in their acquisitions department. We would buy back franchises that were struggling, install new leadership and try to get the franchises back on their feet. Basically, my job was to go around the country telling people that they were fired.

That was a *horrible* job.

I eventually became a KFC Area Manager in Texas. I really wanted to become a district manager, but another guy was promoted over me. I wish I could say that it was a racial thing, but he was Black as well. He was just smarter than me and had been with the company longer than me.

I did always recognize that there was racial discrimination in the workplace. But I also knew that I could break all barriers and do everything I needed to do with determination and hard work. That might sound naïve, but it is what I believed. I had a Notre Dame degree. Therefore, everyone was going to know what I was about.

I did enjoy being an area manager with KFC. I worked at Kentucky Fried Chicken for a long time. I liked being based out of Texas. It was a good place for Sandra and I to raise our family. I also traveled all around for work and had a lot of fun with the job.

CHAPTER 22

I have talked about the good and the bad in my life. Now, I have to talk about the ugly. I would prefer not to talk about it, but it needs to be said. It changed my whole life.

Here's the deal. In the 1990s, I was incarcerated for four and a half years.

My road to prison began with me trying to do something good and selfless. That was followed by regret and then one screw up after another.

While Sandra and I were living with our children in Dallas, Texas, a woman came to stay with us. She was struggling with a lot of things at the time, and Sandra and I were trying to help her out.

We did what we could, but it was not enough. A member of the woman's family came to tragic harm. In the aftermath, there were legal repercussions. Someone would have to answer for the negligent crime.

The woman who we were trying to help was very young. I could not stand the thought of her life being ruined. So, I took the rap for what she had done.

In some ways, it seems like a scene out of, "A Tale of Two Cities" by Charles Dickens. And maybe it was heroic, or noble, or brave, or whatever you want to call it.

Here is the truth, though. I took the fall for the wrong reasons. I did it because I thought I was a bigshot. I thought it was a big thing to do because I was Eric Penick and Eric Penick does things like that. Eric Penick looks after everyone.

Those are the wrong reasons to do something. But one thing led to another, and I confessed to a crime that I did not commit.

Sandra did not like what I had done. She was *pissed off* at what I had done. Sandra was always accepting of a lot of things about me. But she felt hurt that I had not discussed what I was going to do with her. I do not want to say that she was bitter because I do not want to put her in a bad light, but she was very, very hurt.

In the aftermath of my choice, I was feeling awful and would get to drinking a lot and would start to think better about what I had done and what I had given up. By that time, it was too late.

The judge at my trial was a man who had gone to Notre Dame.

The judge asked, "Are you *the* Eric Penick?"

"Yes, sir," I said.

I would have liked to say: "Are you kidding me? You do not know who the hell I am when you are sentencing me to be locked up?"

The judge did not send me directly to prison. He wanted to give me a chance to turn my life around. He sentenced me to what is called, "Shock Probation." I was to spend 180 days in jail. Upon my release, I would be on probation for a period of time and pay numerous fines.

Before I was locked up, I sent Sandra and the kids to live with my mother in Cleveland.

I spent 180 days in jail. When I got out, I went home.

Being in jail for 180 days had not taught me a lesson. I was still drinking a lot and partying and being stupid Eric.

I got to feeling very angry and bitter and sorry for myself about the terms of my probation and the fines I was having to pay. I did not want to do what everyone was telling me I had to do.

One night, I just said, "The hell with it."

Against the terms of my parole, I left Texas and went to Ohio. I gathered Sandra and my kids, and we moved to Michigan.

One of the truths about life is that you can change your location easily enough, but changing yourself is quite a bit more difficult. If you are being stupid, you are going to get yourself into trouble.

I was still hardheaded and doing what I wanted to do and doing it my way. I continued drinking and partying and doing things that I should not do.

Looking back, I think a lot of my drinking came from being

disappointed in myself and my life. I had had a good business career, but it was not the life I was supposed to have lived. I was mad about that. I could not play football anymore. I could not run track anymore. My fractured ankle still hurt all the time. That is no excuse, but that is where I was mentally. I tried to solve my problems with liquor.

One night, after drinking, I got behind the wheel of my car.

I was pulled over and arrested on a Driving While Intoxicated charge (DWI).

While there may have been some nobility in taking the rap for my first conviction, there was no high ground on which to stand for my drunk driving charge. My life was just one big screw up after another. I kept screwing up, and screwing up, and screwing up.

I was found guilty of drunk driving.

What is wild is that the judge in Michigan was from Notre Dame as well. He did perhaps the best thing anyone has ever done for me and sentenced me to prison.

"Mr. Penick, you're going to kill yourself, or somebody else," the judge said. "I'm going to send you to prison because probation didn't work."

I went to the State penitentiary in Michigan.

During that year, a Notre Dame connection once again looked out for me. The house my family and I had moved into in Michigan was owned by a Notre Dame graduate. While I was in prison, Sandra and the kids had no money coming in. My Notre Dame friend did not increase the rent, or kick my family out onto the street. He let them live in the house and looked out for my family.

In the 1960s, when author Ken Kesey was convicted on a marijuana charge, the judge famously called him, "a tarnished Galahad."

Sitting in a prison cell in Michigan, I did not feel like the football hero who had scored an 85-yard touchdown to break open the game against USC. I did not feel like the star who had plunged into the end zone against Alabama to help Notre Dame win the National Championship. I felt like a tarnished failure.

I spent a year of my life in that Michigan prison.

When the year was up, I thought I was going to be free. I had served my time, and I thought I would be able to start my life again.

I was wrong.

In moving with my family to Michigan, I had violated the terms of my probation. There was a Governor's Warrant out for me from the State of Texas

Instead of going home to my family, someone from the Texas Department of Corrections picked me up at the penitentiary in Michigan and drove me down to prison in Texas.

I would be incarcerated in Texas for another three years.

That was truly the best thing that ever happened to me. God had been trying to get my attention all my life. But I was bitter, and I was not listening to Him. During my time in the Texas prison system, God finally got my attention.

It was a roundabout way to get my life back, but going to prison was when I learned that God was in my life.

CHAPTER 23

In prison, I was living in an isolated world with a bunch of crazies.

How fitting then, that it was in that world that I had my apotheosis. I found my peace and my purpose in life while in prison. I had had the answer to living a good and happy life all along. It was not until I got to prison, though, that I started doing what my mother and grandmother had always told me to do: Devote myself to God.

My grandmother and I used to read the bible together. I went to Baptist church with my grandmother and Catholic church with my mother. And then, I moved away from home. I stopped reading my bible. I stopped going to church. I was smoking and drinking and chasing women and doing things I had no business doing. But God has always been there with me. I can tell you that he was always there.

Inside of prison, my journey toward walking with God happened both in steps and all at once.

The first step happened in Michigan.

My first cellmate was a guy who was there for doing some kind of protest, though, I am not sure exactly what his story was. I did find out that he was a Christian and a preacher. He read from the bible with me two or three times. Then, suddenly, he was transferred. I started reading my bible after he was transferred. It seems unusual now that I would have been put in a cell with a Christian preacher for only a few days before they transferred him. I think it was part of God's plan for me, though. God wanted me to take a first step back toward Him.

I continued reading my bible more and more, and I began

praying even more. I was trying to understand what God wanted me to do with my life.

The next thing you know, I was reading my bible every day and praying all the time. I would sing the hymn, "Amazing Grace," while I was mopping the prison floor during my work detail. When I was lifting weights out in the yard, I used to say to myself, "God, power, spirit, and might." I repeated that, "God, power, spirit, and might, God, power, spirit, and might," over and over as I pumped iron, growing stronger in both body and soul.

I had started to be more like who God wanted me to be. Who I was supposed to be!

When I was released from prison in Michigan, I was stunned and heartbroken that I was being sent down to Texas to serve time for breaking the conditions of my parole. But, there again, it was part of God's plan for me.

In the Texas prison system, the inmates would have bible study every Wednesday and Sunday. I soon began leading the bible study and eventually became a preacher for other inmates.

As I started preaching, everything started changing. Locked inside a prison, I was living a beautiful life.

I made a lot of friends. I became a chaplain's assistant. I had found my calling, and the prison system recognized the value I had to offer other inmates.

One day, as life in prison was starting to drain me, and all I could think about was getting to go home, I fell to my knees, and I prayed.

"God, I want to go home," I said. "But, God, however long you want me to be here, however long you want me to stay, I'm going to stay."

The very next day, one of the guards walked by me and said, "Head on tight." That was an order you were given when you were to be transferred.

Someone had given a big decision-maker really good feedback about me. That decision-maker decided to start moving me around the Texas prison system so I could reach more inmates with what I had to say.

That day, I began my journey within the prison system. It was phenomenal. I wound up spending time in four or five different prison units throughout the state. I found out that I could touch people with my message about God.

God was always showing me something. When I decided to let God be in charge of my life, I realized that his grace and blessings were there for me.

There were some really beautiful moments during my time as a preacher in prison.

One year, a bunch of inmates were gathered around the cafeteria to have Thanksgiving Dinner.

Before we started, I stood up and said, "Let's all hold hands and pray."

At that time, I was lifting weights like you would not believe. I was a big, strong guy. I did not worry at all about people thinking I was a little chump for wanting everyone to hold hands.

And in that cafeteria, about 50 guys, Christians, Muslims, atheists, and men with any number of other beliefs, all held hands as I said a prayer before we ate. It might have been against protocol, but the prison guards let us do it.

I knew God was involved in that moment.

In the last prison unit that I was in, called LeBlanc Unit in Beaumont, Texas, I met a man named Garland. He was the warden of the prison, and he became one of my best friends. He is retired now, but I still talk to him to this day.

I ministered to everyone who wanted to listen to my message: Black, White, Latin, Asian, Middle Eastern, everyone. I worked with everyone because I knew that is what God would want me to do.

One guy who took my message to heart was a White man who was part of the Arian Brotherhood. He could not really read, so I helped teach him to read, using the bible. He was worried that someone would find out he was tight with a Black man.

"It's OK," I told him. "No one has to know we're friends. I don't care."

Once, I was asked to talk about business to a group of Muslims. I had my doubts about doing it, but when I wakened that morning, I knew it was what God wanted me to do.

Before I began my business lecture, I knew that I needed to address the religious elephant in the room.

"I'm not going to stand here before you and tell you why my beliefs are right and your beliefs are wrong," I said. "In Matthew 10:33 of the bible, it says that, 'Whoever denies me before men, I will deny before my Father who is in heaven.' So, I will tell you that I am a Christian, and I love God. But the bible also says that God is God of all."

"*Alhamdulilah*," someone said. And then everyone repeated it. "*Alhamdulilah*. Praise be to God."

Being around so many different religions inside of prison, I learned that God is with everybody. I used to tell the Muslims, "If you're truly a Muslim, and you truly pray all the time, then serve your God, Allah.

In prison, I began to identify as Nondenominational. I took the best things from my Baptist and Catholic upbringing, along with some things from other religions and made my relationship with God truly my own.

I remember that I used to look up at the sky all the time. I would think about being away from my family and I would say, "God, I know we're all looking at the same sky. And please God, please God, let my wife and kids know that I love them." And I knew that God was contacting them through my prayer.

Before prison, my belief system was based on talking to a priest. And I could talk to a man, but it was very different talking to God. Of course, I still talked through men, but as my belief system grew, and as I grew in God, I learned to really love talking to God.

There were also some really damn scary moments in prison. There were riots and all kinds of violent fights.

I hated that stuff going on around me and was never involved. I remember in one of my first units in Texas, I was in the cafeteria and I saw things starting to bubble over between some of the guys around me. I turned to a friend and said, "We need to get out of here. Now."

My buddy and I had just gotten out of the cafeteria when a full-blown riot began.

Other times, I was not so lucky and would get caught in the wrong place at the wrong time. I can still remember lying on the ground as the guards were trying to secure a riot.

There were a lot of gangs in the prisons. I used to tell the gangs that they could not conduct gang business within the chapel where I was preaching. I used to talk with the heads of the gangs and bargain with them for the guys who wanted to get out of the gangs.

It was scary as hell. A man alone cannot beat a gang. If a gang decides they are going to whoop your butt with coins in a sock, you are going to be whooped. It is that simple. But I knew I had to stand up before those gangs. And I knew I could do it. Not because I was strong in body, but because I was strong in Christ.

I spent three years preaching within the Texas prison system. I met a lot of people, and I know that I touched a lot of lives. I always wanted to serve God more and more every day.

When I tell people that I spent time in prison, I always say that it was a horrible thing, but it was not a bad thing.

God had a plan for my life all along. No matter how screwed up I got, God made sure that He took care of me. That is what is important. The bottom line is that God has always, always looked after me in my life. God has always, always been there for me no matter what. No matter what I did right or what I did wrong, no matter how good or bad I have been, God has always been there.

When I was running track, God was making me a champion. When I was playing football, God was making me a champion.

When I got sent to prison, God made me a Man of God and a preacher.

God was just always looking out for me. Always.

CHAPTER 24

After four and a half years spent inside jail and prison walls, I walked out a free man.

While going to prison may have changed my life for the better, there were still consequences to be paid.

I missed out on four and a half years with my wife and our children. By the time I got out, my youngest was eight-years-old and had started school. My oldest was already in high school.

It felt good to be out of prison, of course. But it was a struggle too. I realized that I could not be friends with some of the people with whom I had been friends before I went to prison. Some of those people were still drinking a lot and leading a lifestyle that I did not want to lead anymore.

While in prison, I quit alcohol and have not touched it since. I knew I just should not drink anymore. I do not believe that I am an alcoholic, but I would drink and bury my feelings in liquor. Since going to prison, I have not had any inclination to do that.

Once I got out of prison, Sandra and my kids were with me again, and that was important. But there was still so much that I had to do.

The first thing was that I had to find a house for my family and me that I could afford. That was not easy since I had such a huge family at that time.

I had to find a job, too.

Eventually, my family and I moved into a place in Dallas.

I applied for a position as a mortgage banker account representative at United Mortgage Company. I got the job and started moving up the ranks. I kept working and working and working until the opportunity to be a district manager came. I moved up to that role, and kept on going until I became the company's Executive Vice President. That was a pinnacle job for me. I made big decisions, hired people, and even bought other mortgage companies.

When I look back at my career trajectory now, I realize that there were many times when I felt upset about my path. I often wondered why I had to fight for promotions and jobs. I wondered why other people got a position that I did not get. Now, I realize that those moments helped me grow and persevere. That was a blessing.

Football, track and school had made me determined to do the best that I could do. In the business world, I decided that if you were blocking my way, I was going to run through you or over you. I would just push forward. Push, push, push. That is how I became an Executive Vice President. I kept pushing. I went out and did better than anyone else and let the chips fall where they may.

In my last job before I retired, I decided to try going out on my own as a businessman. A friend of mine named Bobby Roan taught me how to buy and sell homes. I really liked the process and after I had learned a lot from Bobby, I started my own company, calling it Stored in Heaven.

It was a fantastic way to make a living. I was getting *paid*. The company would buy homes, fix them up and then sell them off to different buyers, including corporations looking to buy numerous houses. It was like a gravy train.

On top of my business ventures, I started preaching at the Dallas Youth Village, a nonsecure residential placement facility for young men who were on a bad path.

I had a story to tell about my life. I used that story to try to change the lives of those young men.

"If you devote yourself to turning your life around, you go through some hard times, but never bad times," I would tell the young men. "Because God is always there. I changed my life inside of prison, and that is a blessing. But you can change your life a lot easier outside of prison than inside prison."

Some of the young men would not listen to me, and they kept

walking down a bad path. Some of them would listen to me, though. It was such a joy to be out eating somewhere and run into one of the young men on whose life I had had an impact. They would come say hi to me, and I would see that they were all grown up and that they had changed the direction of their lives.

I had suffered a lot, but I was finally leading a good life, the kind of life I had always wanted for myself.

CHAPTER 25

My suffering was not over, though.

After 37-years of marriage, Sandra got sick.

Sandra was such a special person. I expected her to be the one to bury me someday. That was not how it worked out, though.

Sandra was a smoker. I always told her that she needed to quit smoking, but she did not.

In 2018, Sandra was diagnosed with lung cancer. They caught it late. Sandra was sick for six months. Six lousy months before she was gone.

Afterward, I just balled up into a shell. And after that, I got old.

My daughter, Jewel, keeps a picture of Sandra on the wall of her house. I am living with Jewel now, and I look at Sandra's picture every day.

Years later, I still love Sandra and feel committed to her. I will always love Sandra and feel committed to her.

CHAPTER 26

In many ways, I was still reeling from Sandra's death when the old ankle injury that had ended my football career became a problem again. This time, that injury nearly ended my life.

As I moved through my 60s, I felt like I was in pretty decent health. The ankle that I had broken at Notre Dame was still a problem. I was a little heavy, but not too heavy. At one time, when I was drinking a lot, I gained the beer weight which I had not gained in college, and I ballooned up to close to 300-pounds. I eventually lost that weight, though. By the time everything caught up with me, I was down to around 220-pounds, only a little heavier than what my playing weight had been. I was active and working out a lot.

My biological father had had diabetes. He died after passing out in the bathroom and hitting his head on the bathtub. My mother died of cancer. The causes of death for my biological parents did not faze me as far as my own health was concerned.

My sister, Mosetta, was diagnosed with diabetes. She told me that given the family history, I needed to get myself checked out. I can be a hardheaded man, though. I hoped that despite the family history, diabetes would just skip me.

It did not.

Early in 2019, my dog, an 80-pound St. Bernard/Mastiff mutt named Zoe, scratched a toe on my left leg. The toe did not heal. Eventually I went to the doctor. That was when they found out that I had Type 1 Diabetes.

The diabetes combined with vascular problems from my broken ankle meant that I was in trouble.

The doctors started chopping me apart.

They cut off my toes first. My vascular system was failing to pump blood into the toes on my left foot. And one-by-one, the doctors amputated my toes.

Even without toes, I was OK. I could put shoes on so no one would notice I was missing part of myself. At first, I had to use a walker to get around. Eventually, though, I was able to start walking again on my own.

When the COVID-19 pandemic began, I moved in with my best friend Mike Clark. I always say that I have best *friends*, not *a* best friend. Mike is one of my best friends. We lived together the whole first year and a half of the pandemic. It was so much fun. We would have barbeque all the time and smoke cigars together every Friday night.

After the pandemic slowed down in Texas, I got my own apartment and my dog Zoe and I started living by ourselves again. I had a housekeeper who would take care of cleaning and grocery shopping and things like that.

I did not have my toes anymore, but I thought I was going to be OK.

Then I got really sick.

One day, my housekeeper came home and found me in bad shape. I was lying on the couch, not able to move. I had urinated all over myself.

"You need to go to the hospital" my housekeeper said. "I need to call an ambulance. Something is wrong with you. You're not talking right. You don't look right."

"No. No. No," I said. "Don't call anyone."

I was delirious, but even in my delirium, I knew that I was Eric Penick. I could get through anything, and I would get better physically all on my own.

The housekeeper finally called my daughter, Jewel. I do not listen to a lot of people, but I actually do listen to Jewel. She talked to me on the phone and convinced me that something was wrong with me physically and mentally. She told me that I needed to go to the hospital. She convinced me, and she saved my life.

I was pretty out of it for most of what happened next.

In the hospital, the doctors tested me to see the extent of my vascular problem. The problem was confined to my left leg. The doctors kept testing me and poking at me and trying to figure out a way to save my leg.

The broken ankle that had never healed right combined with diabetes was a disastrous combination.

I do not remember a whole lot else. I was totally out of it. Jewel came to Dallas to be with me. I had other friends come see me. I may have interacted with Jewel and my other friends, but I only learned about how everyone had come to see me later when I was told about it.

When I really woke up and understood what was going on, I was horrified. The doctors had amputated my left leg, above my knee.

"What the hell?" I said aloud, looking down at where my leg had been.

I had not wanted to go to the hospital in the first place. And I had been made to go anyway, and now, I did not have a leg. I was mad at the world and everybody in it. Are you kidding me? I was pissed at the world and everybody living in it.

I wound up spending seven months in hospitals. I stayed in the hospital where they had amputated my leg for a while. Eventually, I was moved to a hospital rehabilitation facility.

I was not in control of anything about my life. My best friend, Eddie Hill, who had gone to Notre Dame with me, helped clean out my apartment. It was obvious I was not going to go back home, and all of my stuff had to be sold or donated: My tv; my couch; my clothes. I did not have anything left by the time I got out of the hospital. Eddie even had to find a new home for Zoe.

I still miss Zoe.

I live with Jewel and her two dogs now, but Zoe was *my* dog. I used to treat Zoe like a human being. My daughter treats her dogs like dogs. I know she loves them, but we treat them like dogs. That was not my style with Zoe. That big 80-pound dog would sit on the couch with me and get right on my lap. I would just hold her and love her.

Lying in hospital beds at night, I would dream that I was

running. More than running on the football field, I dreamed about running track. I always was a track man. I dreamed about running every time I fell asleep in the hospital. I was just always dreaming about running.

When I wakened, I would look down and see that I no longer had a leg. I used to beg the doctors to shoot me up with drugs so that I could go back to sleep and dream again. I did not want to face the reality of no longer having a leg.

In June of 2022, I was discharged from the hospital rehabilitation facility. I could no longer live by myself. I was looking into moving into a Medicare subsidized assisted living home when Jewel asked me to move in with her in Michigan.

In Michigan, Jewel took me to every doctor imaginable.

I was fitted for a prosthetic leg.

My teeth were ruined by diabetes, and the dentist wound up having to pull all of them, except for the two front teeth I had had replaced after getting them knocked out against Pitt. I was in the dentist's office for about three hours. The dentist was just grinding, cutting, grinding, cutting and then stitching up my mouth.

That *really* sucked.

I was put on a plan to manage my diabetes. Shockingly, I was told that it could be kept under control without insulin if I was meticulous about my diet, which I have been. I am hungry a lot, but I only eat what I am allowed to eat.

Slowly, I have been regaining my health. I am a running back and track star without a leg, though. I feel like I am half a man half the time.

In the darkest days of my sickness, after my leg had been cut off, I used to want to die.

Now, though, I have things to focus on. I have reasons to make myself strong so that I can continue living.

CHAPTER THE LAST

I have been living in Grand Blanc, Michigan since June of 2022. Grand Blanc is a suburb of Flint, the home turf of my former Notre Dame teammate Reggie Barnett.

Jewel welcomed me into her home and I now share it with her, and her family, including two of my grandchildren, my granddaughter Kaylynn and my grandson Kaeson.

As of July 2023, I am still struggling with my health somewhat, but nothing like I was before. I am going to physical therapy five times a week and getting better as far as getting around. The physical therapists are really rough on me. They put me through all kinds of exercises and try to kill me every time I see them. But I always tell them, "Thank you," at the end of my sessions because they have motivated me to continue progressing. That makes my day.

My diabetes is under control through my diet. I would love to be able to eat more food, because I am always hungry, but I know the healthy diet is keeping me alive.

The physical trauma I experienced took a toll on me mentally, but my mind is getting sharper every day.

One of the ways I have been trying to sharpen my mind is by continuing to read my scripture.

I start each morning by reading scripture for 15 or 20 minutes. I have read the bible three or four times all the way through. Now, I use an app on my phone, which is really cool. My favorite times are when the app pops up verses from Psalms. I love reading anything from Psalms.

Just today, I read Psalm 37:25, which seemed particularly meaningful: "I have been young, and now am old; Yet I have not seen the righteous forsaken."

Scripture verses like that, which have a really deep meaning toward my life are very, very important to me.

Really, though, I enjoy any scripture verse. I can always take something about it into my day. I read the verse and then I sit with myself for a time, trying to absorb what I just read.

I finish each day by praying myself to sleep. I try to pray for every person I know. And I know a lot of people. There are the eight kids; all of the grandkids, up through my great granddaughter; all of the cousins on both my mother and father's side; all the friends I have made over the years. I say the name of each person and pray for them, praying for the covenant of the blood of Jesus on all of them.

At the end of my prayer, I always say, "Love God with all your heart, and all your mind, and all your soul. And love thy neighbor as yourself."

Sometimes I go slow, and sometimes I can feel myself falling asleep so I have to go quickly. It is fun, though. I enjoy talking to God about the people in my life. And all of my friends know that when I say, "I'll pray for you," I am not just saying it. I really will pray for them. And of course, it means so much to me to know that I have friends who are praying for me as well.

I need those prayers because I still have so much that I want to do with my life. I am almost 70-years-old, but I still have dreams. When you are young you are supposed to have dreams, right? Well, I do not believe you should stop having dreams just because you get old.

Just like after Sandra died, I look forward to motivate myself.

I have some business ventures that I would like to start again. When I was younger, I thought being retired was going to be cool. Well, now that I am retired, I can tell you it is not cool at all. I loved buying and selling houses in Texas, and I could see myself trying to do that again in Michigan.

What I would really love to do is start preaching again. I need to get a little better at moving around, and I need my mind to continue improving and getting sharper. I still have a lot to say, and I know I can still touch people's lives with my message about

God.

I believe that being a preacher is something God wants me to do. And I would feel blessed to be able to talk to the people with whom God wants me to talk.

I have a lot of physical goals too. I do not just want to walk and get about on my prosthetic leg.

I dream about running. That is the goal I work toward every time I go to physical therapy. I want to be strong enough to get a racing prosthetic blade and do the 100-yard-dash again. If I am going to run, I want to get down into my starting blocks, and I want to sprint.

I do not know in what time I could run the 100-yard-dash. Maybe 15 seconds, maybe 20-seconds, maybe it would take me a whole hour. I just want to be able to do it. It would not be about winning a race, or how fast I could run. It would be about saying that I wanted to run the 100-yard-dash, and knowing that I ran it.

And do you know what? If I ran against other 70-year-old guys, and if I was in shape, I think I could win the race. I still have that belief in myself. I believe in my ability to accomplish things. I believe that God will make my dreams real.

In many ways, my life has been defined by my runs. Running track in high school, I won an unprecedented five Ohio State Championships in the sprints. Running the ball for Notre Dame, I got into the end zone at some of most crucial moments of our 1973 National Championship season. Later, I found myself running away from the man who I was supposed to be. Then I ran from the law and found myself in prison. While incarcerated, though, I began running back toward God. Now, I continue to dream of getting onto a track and running again even without my leg. And every day, I run to embrace each waking moment. I run to be a force of good for my family, which includes every teammate I had at Gilmour Academy and Notre Dame.

Because of that, I always have something to look forward to when I wake up each morning.

As long as that remains true, I have nothing to worry about. Because, you see, I am no longer afraid to die.

I know that if I continue to live my life properly and believe in Christ, and walk the narrow path, that I am going to see God one day. I am going to be with Jesus. Dying is inevitable. But I love God with all my heart, and all my soul, and all my being, and I love my neighbor as myself. I understand that my love for God and my obedience to Him will bring me to the Kingdom of Heaven.

There, I will see all the people I met in this life who passed before me. My mother and father will be there. So will my grandmother and all my aunts and uncles and cousins. I will see my friends. I will see all the guys I played football against, and all my teammates. Coach Parseghian will be there too.

In heaven, I will have both of my legs again. Maybe I will have the body I had 50-years ago, when I was scoring an 85-yard touchdown to break open the game against USC, or running in a touchdown against Alabama to help Notre Dame win the National Championship. Maybe I will not have a body at all. The bottom line is that I will be happy. I will exist in joy. I will walk with the Lord.

And just maybe, if He deems it, I will run with the Lord.

EPILOGUE

I wrote this book so that all of my grandchildren could learn my story. I want them to know what my life was like. I want them to see the mistakes I made so they do not make the same ones. I also want them to see my triumphs so that they know what they are capable of.

As I turn 70-years-old, and as the 50th anniversary of Notre Dame's 1973 National Championship approaches, I also thought that it was time to tell my story. A lot of people think that Eric Penick was such a great guy. I wanted to tell everyone about the rest of my life, and show them what I went through to become who I am today.

For a long time, I did not think much about football. I used to go to Notre Dame games every so often and tailgate with friends. Those games were more social experiences than anything.

I think about football a lot now, though, because I do not have a leg.

Throughout my life, there were a lot of bad things that happened to me and a lot mistakes were made. Life is full of negatives, though. There were also a lot of good things that happened to me and things that I accomplished.

When I think back about my life, the successes I had were because everybody pushed me. At the time, I thought, "What a bunch of shit. Why do I have to work so hard for this, or work so hard for that?"

In the beginning, everything was so easy for me. Track, football, school, everything. But in real life, people must strive and work for what they want. I had to learn how to do that. I really understand now, all the different struggles and all the different things that I had to go through, it was all developing me as a person.

I am still developing as a person. I am trying to relearn how to walk now. I have to work hard at it. My arms are always tired. My one leg gets tired. I feel beaten up and just tired all the time. But I keep pushing. I persevere to be better. I persevere to be the best that I can be.

Ara Parseghian passed away on August 2, 2017 at 94-years-old. I think back often to the conversations I had long ago with my coach.

"Coach," I said, "what kind of man will I be when I leave Notre Dame?"

"I don't know right now, Eric," Coach Parseghian said. "You haven't had any adversity in your life. Everything has been handed to you. Everything has been good for you. I can tell you about the guys who aren't playing and what kind of guys they are. But you, I just don't know yet."

And then, I went through adversity. I lost football. I lost my freedom. And finally, I lost my leg.

Through it all, though, I rose again and again. I walked straight through hell so that I could feel the light of heaven upon my face.

Ara saw that.

"Eric," Coach Parseghian told me, years later, "I can see it now. Before, I didn't know what kind of man you would be because you always had it made as a football player, and in life. I can see the adversity you went through now, though. You learned how to persevere in good times and bad times. Now, I can tell what kind of a man you are by the obstacles you've overcome. I know what kind of man you are, Eric. You are a good man."

Ara had always taught us that only through adversity did our best qualities emerge. Qualities that would have otherwise remained dormant.

Coach Parseghian was right. It was the adversity that I went through which brought out the best in me and turned me into the man that I am today. In the end, I became a good man.

I will always be a Notre Dame Man.

The End

ACKNOWLEDGEMENTS

This book reveals an extraordinary life. But life never stops moving forward. As the authors worked on this book, they experienced joy and tragedy, birth and death, triumphs and setbacks. At separate times, both Eric and Stephen found themselves calling each other to continue working on this book while in a hospital, holding vigil for a loved one. Through it all, the authors continued meeting regularly to work on this book. They became not only friends, but family.

The authors wish to extend their sincere gratitude to some of the people who helped make this book possible:

Eric's daughter Jewel for taking amazing care of him.

All of Eric's children, grandchildren, friends and family for their love and support.

Stephen's wife, Sarah, and daughter, Morgan, for giving him uninterrupted time to research, organize and write this book.

Jennifer Kellogg for being the best aunt to Morgan while you were here and watching over Morgan now that you are gone.

Dave Casper, for writing his heart-felt Foreword.

Drew Mahalic for his editorial work and for recognizing that Eric's unique story needed to be shared with all sports fans, athletes at every level and their parents.

James T. "Brad" Bradley for graciously providing the cover photo of Eric.

Gilmour Academy for research and providing the back photo of Eric.

The great Notre Dame running back, Al Samuel, for always being there for Eric and calling him every single day.

Mike Clark, Eric's cigar smoking buddy, for being his friend and supporting him during the pandemic.

Eddie Hill and Mike Keating for connecting generations of Notre Dame football players.

Notre Dame Assistant Athletics Director Hunter Bivin for being an advocate and champion for this book.

Cappy Gagnon for his extraordinary ability to find Notre Dame football stats.

Mike Steele for his insight into navigating the world of Notre Dame football.

Jim Lefebvre for his suggestions on how to make this book a success.

Jason Vondersmith for knowing whether a comma should be included or not.

ABOUT THE AUTHORS

Eric Penick

Eric Penick was born in Cleveland, Ohio. He was a superstar sprinter and running back at Gilmour Academy. He went on to become a legendary tailback for the Notre Dame Fighting Irish from 1972-1974. Eric is immortalized in Irish lore for his game-breaking 85-yard touchdown run against USC in 1973, and his pivotal touchdown run against Alabama in the 1973 Sugar Bowl which helped Notre Dame win the 1973 National Championship. He lives in Grand Blanc, Michigan with his daughter Jewel and his grandchildren. Eric is a Notre Dame Man.

Stephen Alexander

Stephen Alexander is a Bestselling author, an award-winning journalist and a senior technical writer. He is the son of Notre Dame starting linebacker Drew Mahalic (1972-74). "A Notre Dame Man: The Life, Lore and Runs of Eric Penick" is Stephen's eighth book. He lives in Portland, Oregon with his wife, Sarah, his daughter, Morgan, and his amazing pug, Gus.

Made in the USA
Middletown, DE
16 October 2023

40940695R00066